Canadian Indian Policy

BIBLIOGRAPHICAL SERIES
*The Newberry Library Center
for the History of the American Indian*

General Editor
Francis Jennings

Assistant Editor
William R. Swagerty

The Center Is Supported by Grants from

The National Endowment for the Humanities
The Ford Foundation
The W. Clement and Jessie V. Stone Foundation
The Woods Charitable Fund, Inc.
Mr. Gaylord Donnelley
The Andrew W. Mellon Foundation
The Robert R. McCormick Charitable Trust
The John D. and Catherine T. McArthur Foundation

Canadian Indian Policy

A Critical Bibliography

ROBERT J. SURTEES

Published for the Newberry Library

Indiana University Press

BLOOMINGTON

Manufactured in the United States of America

Library of Congress Cataloging in Publication Data

Surtees, Robert J., 1941–
    Canadian Indian policy.

    (Bibliographical series / The Newberry Library Center for the History of the American Indian)
    Includes index.
    1. Indians of North America—Canada—Government relations—Bibliography. I. Title. II. Series: Bibliographical series (Newberry Library. Center for the History of the American Indian)
    Z1209.2.C2S9 [E92]   016.3231'197'071   81–48088
    ISBN 0–253–31300—7 (pbk.)   AACR2
    1 2 3 4 5 86 85 84 83 82

CONTENTS

Maps

RECOMMENDED WORKS

For the Beginner

[7] Anglican Church of Canada, *Bulletin 201.*

[15] R. P. Bowes et al., *The Indian: Assimilation, Integration or Separation?*

[33] Canada, Department of Indian Affairs and Northern Development, *Atlas of Indian Reserves and Settlements, Canada 1971.*

[46] Harold Cardinal, *The Unjust Society.*

[74] Wilson Duff, *The Indian History of British Columbia.*

[78] Jean Leonard Elliott, ed. *Minority Canadians,* Vol. 1. *Native Peoples.*

[183] E. Palmer Patterson II, *The Canadian Indian: A History since 1500.*

[228] Norma Sluman, *Poundmaker.*

[237] George F. G. Stanley, "The Indian Background to Canadian History."

[246] Robert J. Surtees, *The Original People.*

[248]   Fraser Symington, *The Canadian Indian.*

For a Basic Library Collection

[4]   Robert S. Allen, *The British Indian Department and the Frontier in North America: 1755–1830.*

[64]   Peter A. Cumming and Neil H. Mickenberg, eds., *Native Rights in Canada.*

[131]   George T. Hunt, *The Wars of the Iroquois.*

[140]   Cornelius J. Jaenen, *Friend and Foe.*

[147]   Charles M. Johnston, *The Valley of the Six Nations.*

[157]   Forrest E. La Violette, *The Struggle for Survival.*

[161]   John Leslie and Ron Maguire, eds., *The Historical Development of the Indian Act.*

[176]   Alexander Morris, *The Treaties of Canada with the Indians.*

[177]   J. L. Morris, *Indians of Ontario.*

[183]   E. Palmer Patterson II, *The Canadian Indian: A History since 1500.*

[239]   George F. G. Stanley, *The Birth of Western Canada*.

[265]   Bruce G. Trigger, *The Children of Aataentsic*.

[274]   Leslie F. S. Upton, *Micmacs and Colonists*.

BIBLIOGRAPHICAL ESSAY

Introduction

Canadian Indian policy has evolved over four centuries. It has involved the positive and passive participation of three distinct regimes — French, British, and Canadian — and has been shaped by factors ranging from the needs of traders to the international balance of power. Yet it is a field of study that has attracted remarkably little attention from historians and other scholars. To date, therefore, there is no comprehensive study that traces this evolution and the circumstances surrounding it. There are, however, numerous monographs, biographies, and general histories that, in dealing with their own topics, provide some analysis of Indian policy at particular periods or in certain circumstances. Gilbert C. Patterson's study of land policy in Upper Canada, for example, includes a chapter on Indian lands [182]. In addition, there are studies of persons or events relating to Indian policy.

This pattern has been more common in the past decade than ever before as graduate students have embarked in a variety of directions within the general area of Indian affairs. The recent interest was sparked, no doubt, by the controversy that surrounded the Canadian government's 1969 White Paper on Indian policy (See below, p. 54), but these efforts have resulted only in a spate of articles or books of very limited scope, and much remains in thesis form. Consequently the literature is uneven. From these widely diverse studies, however, despite the range in the quality of the work, a fairly complete general picture can be drawn.

Some preliminary efforts have already been made. George F. G. Stanley, who has pioneered several avenues into Canadian history, provides an outline—in very general terms—of Indian policy over the course of three regimes in "The Indian Background to Canadian History" [237], and E. Palmer Patterson II gives a general assessment of policy in his attempt to examine Indian-White relations in *The Canadian Indian: A History since 1500* [183]. My own *The Original People* [246], designed for use in secondary schools, also highlights the evolving policy since the sixteenth century. The most recent similar effort is the chapter "A History of Indian-Government Relations" in J. Rick Ponting and Roger Gibbins, *Out of Irrelevance: A Socio-political Introduction to Indian Affairs in Canada* [188]. This work concentrates on the Canadian era, as does John L. Tobias's "Protection, Civilization, Assimilation: An Outline History of Canada's Indian Policy" [252]. Mention should also be made of *Canadian Indians and the Law: Selected Documents, 1663–1972* [229], edited by Derek G. Smith, a carefully planned and highly useful collection of the major documents concerning the constitutional and legal nature of Indian affairs in Canada. *Native Rights in Canada*, 2d edition, edited by Peter A. Cumming and Neil H. Mickenburg [64], bears noting as well, for it is the most ambitious, and most complete, general treatment of Indian affairs and Indian policy that currently exists.

Although this volume is concerned with policy, certain general studies concerning the Indians of Canada must be mentioned. Diamond Jenness's *The Indians of Canada* [143], first issued in 1932, remains the most useful one-volume study. Also still valuable is the *Handbook of Indians of Canada* [39], first published in 1913 by the Geographic Board of Canada and reprinted in 1971 by the Coles Publishing Company. A French edition was issued in 1915. Four articles from the extensive writings of Jacques Rousseau are also recommended: "Du bon sauvage de la littérature à celui de la realité" [206]; "Ces gens qu'on dit sauvages" [207]; "Les sachems déliberent autour du feu de camp" [208]; and "Les premiers canadiens" [209]. Alfred G. Bailey's *The Conflict of European and Eastern Algonkian Cultures 1504–1700* [8], first issued in 1937 and reprinted in 1969, is a classic account of the opening years of Indian-White contact.

The most complete bibliography concerning the Indians of Canada is that by Don Whiteside, *Aboriginal People: A Selected Bibliography concerning Canada's First People* [285]. Donald B. Smith's bibliographical essay in *Le Sauvage* [230] is also very valuable. The general historiography of Indian affairs was nicely treated in James Walker's 1971 essay, "The Indian in Canadian Historical Writing" [278]. And, of course, several titles in this series of bibliographies are relevant to Canadian Indians, including the following: Helen Hornbeck Tanner, *The Ojibwas* [249]; June Helm, *The Indians of the Subarctic* [115]; E. Adamson Hoebel, *The Plains In-*

dians [122]; C. A. Weslager, *The Delawares* [284]; Elizabeth Tooker, *The Indians of the Northeast* [256]; Robert S. Grumet, *Native Americans of the Northwest Coast* [106]; and James P. Ronda and James Axtell, *Indian Missions* [205].

The French Period: 1608–1763

Introduction

After a century of casual contact with the Indians, in 1608 the French finally established themselves permanently at Quebec on the Saint Lawrence River. At that time they were outnumbered and existed largely at the sufferance of the Algonquin Indians who surrounded them. By the end of the century the French had extended their fur trading enterprises to claim a nominal sovereignty over the Great Lakes basin and into the Mississippi Valley, and a half-century later the French empire in North America extended to the Rocky Mountains in the west and to the mouth of the Mississippi River. They were, however, still outnumbered by the several tribes of Indians who continued to surround their settlements, forts, and trading posts. And to a large extent they were still in possession of that territory at the sufferance of the Indians.

Throughout the French regime, therefore, relations between the French and their Indian neighbors were vitally important and often extremely delicate. The policy the French pursued toward the Indians was

dictated by this prevailing factor, but it was also determined by the Frenchmen's European and Catholic
background, and by the various views they had of the
Indians. The result was a policy of expediency mixed
with evangelical fervor and a sense of cultural
superiority. The latter, of course, could not be permitted to surface too blatantly in circumstances where the
French position was weak; yet weakness could not be
permitted to become too discernible either, for that
could alienate alliances. The French had to travel a
very precarious road when dealing with the Indians,
and the path very often was deceptive to the observer.

Francis Parkman apparently was one observer who
was deceived. At one point in his monumental writings
he observed that "Spanish civilization crushed the Indian; English civilization scorned and neglected him;
French civilization embraced and cherished him." And
indeed that is an impression one gets from observing
the way French traders, soldiers, and priests seemed to
work with the Indians in extending the French fur
trading and imperial activities. It was, in fact, an impression the French themselves were pleased to promote, as Cornelius Jaenen notes in the introduction to
his prizewinning *Friend and Foe: Aspects of French-
Amerindian Cultural Contact in the Sixteenth and Seventeenth Centuries* [140] (p. 7). Jaenen refutes the argu-
ment that the French were more inclined to befriend
the Indian than were other European races. His book
cites examples of cultural clashes between the French
and the Indians that reveal that the French considered

the Indians vagabonds and barbarians even after they had adopted Christianity. His article "The Meeting of the French and Amerindians in the Seventeenth Century" [138] provides a briefer summary on the same theme. Other accounts that deal with the French image of the Indians include George R. Healy, "The French Jesuits and the Idea of the Noble Savage" [113], J. H. Kennedy, *Jesuit and Savage in New France* [150], and Gilbert Chinard's *L'Amérique et le rêve exotique dans la littérature francaise au dix-septième et au dix-huitième siècle* [49]. A unique study is Donald B. Smith, *Le Sauvage: The Native People in Quebec Historical Writing on the Heroic Period (1534–1633) of New France* [230]. This book is very satisfying on the basis of its own theme, the examination of the image of Indians portrayed by French and French Canadian historians, but it is also valuable for its allusions to policy. It ends with an excellent essay, "The Native People of Southern Quebec: An Historical Bibliography."

Despite their feelings of superiority, however, the French had to remain circumspect because of their tenuous position. Over the course of the French regime in Canada, they pursued three major activities: the fur trade, missionary work, and, after 1701, an active imperialism. All three were blended, and all three depended upon the assistance and cooperation of the Indians. This dependence was apparent from the first days of the Quebec settlement.

French-Iroquois-Huron Relations

The prime motive for the French presence in Canada was the commercial advantage to be wrought from the fur trade, and this consideration forced the French into arrangements with the Algonquins of the Saint Lawrence Valley and with the Hurons and other Iroquois (Neutrals and Petuns) north of Lake Erie. A secondary motive, but a highly important one, was the missionary activity among the Indians. Indeed, as Olive P. Dickason points out in her *Louisbourg and the Indians* [72], the French adopted conversion as an official goal as early as 1540 (p. 19). It was logical that this activity should begin among the Indians who supplied the French with furs—the Algonquins and the Hurons. As it evolved, this trading and missionary work set the French at odds with the Five Nations Confederacy, and that in turn began a long series of wars with the Iroquois. These three themes of early French-Indian relations—trade, conversion, and Iroquois conflicts—are discussed in Bruce Trigger's fine article "Champlain Judged by His Indian Policy: A Different View of Early Canadian History" [263]. Trigger also demonstrates the precarious position of the French in those early years by describing Champlain's difficulties in asserting his authority over the Montagnais bands in the region of Quebec.

The same article discusses the origins of the French-Iroquois conflict and rejects the once-accepted view that it was caused by Champlain's forays against

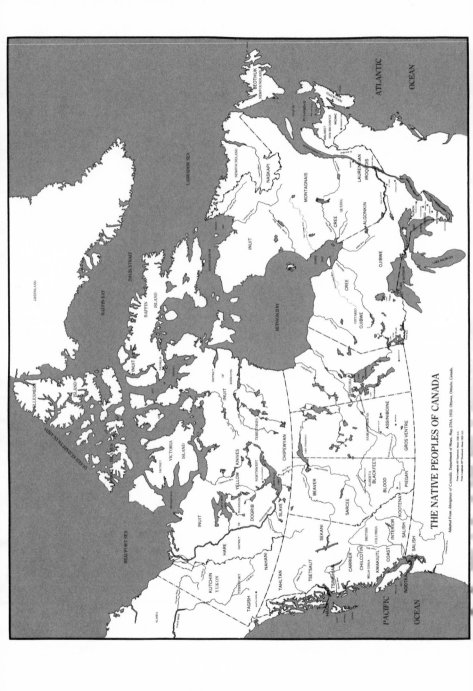

THE NATIVE PEOPLES OF CANADA

Adapted From: Aborigines of Canada. Department of Mines, Map 270A, 1932. Ottawa, Ontario, Canada.

the Iroquois in 1609 and 1615. The Iroquois were prepared to overlook those actions in the interests of commerce, and the French were also willing to preach and trade in Iroquois centers. Efforts were made in this regard, such as Father Jogues's missions to the Iroquois, but they usually proved unsuccessful. Factors of geography, intertribal traditional rivalries and commerce, as well as the appearance of the Dutch on the Hudson River, required that the French reject the Iroquois as trading allies and cultivate the partnership of the Hurons and Algonquins of Canada. The commercial aspects of intertribal rivalries and the French-Iroquois conflicts have been traced brilliantly in George T. Hunt's *The Wars of the Iroquois* [131]. This volume first appeared in 1940, but since then its emphasis on trade and commerce has been modified. It remains an essential source, although the researcher is cautioned not to accept many of Hunt's "facts." Robert A. Goldstein also covers the warfare in his *French-Iroquois Diplomatic and Military Relations, 1609–1701* [96]. On early French-Iroquois-Huron relations, Leo-Paul Derosiers, *Iroquoisie*, volume 1, *1534–1646* [71] remains an excellent summary. Peter G. LeBlanc's "Indian-Missionary Contact in Huronia, 1615–1649" [159] nicely surveys that subject.

Few topics in Canadian history have received as much attention as the Huron-French relationships of the first half of the seventeenth century. The work of Bruce Trigger in particular stands out. His most recent offering, a masterly two-volume study entitled *The*

Children of Aataentsic: A History of the Huron People to 1660 [265], will no doubt remain the most important source concerning the Hurons for some time to come. Admiration for *The Children of Aataentsic*, however, should not preclude reference to other fine studies, including Elizabeth Tooker, *An Ethnography of the Huron Indians, 1615–1649* [255], and Conrad Heidenreich, *Huronia: A History and Geography of the Huron Indians, 1600–1650* [114], which won the Saint Marie prize for 1972. Elizabeth Tooker's "The Iroquois Defeat of the Huron" [254] should be consulted for an explanation of the Iroquois victory over the Hurons. Trigger's work is extensive, but special attention is drawn to the following: "The Historic Location of the Hurons" [260]; "The French Presence in Huronia: The Structure of Franco-Huron Relations in the First Half of the Seventeenth Century" [262]; "The Jesuits and the Fur Trade" [261]; "The Destruction of Huronia: A Study in Economic and Cultural Change, 1609–1650" [259]; and "The Mohawk-Mahican War (1624–28)" [264].

Policy of "Francization"

Huronia was destroyed in 1649; the Iroquois wars continued until the end of the century; and the French, in addition to strengthening their Saint Lawrence base somewhat, extended their activities westward. Concurrent with the last twenty years of activities in Huronia, and extending till late in the seventeenth century, the French civil and religious authorities adopted a program of civilization as well as conversion as their official Indian policy. The first historian to examine this policy, in isolation, was George F. G. Stanley, who broached the subject in a 1949 article, "The Policy of 'Francisation' as Applied to the Indians during the Ancien Régime" [234]. He followed this with two related articles, "The First Indian 'Reserves' in Canada" [235], and "The Indians and the Brandy Trade during the Ancien Régime" [238]. In the first of these, Stanley explained how the Jesuits attempted to convince the Indians to adopt the French life-style, the French mores, and the French religion through the use of boarding schools. Later the civil authorities, refusing to accept the Jesuit failures as an indicator of the policy's lack of validity, promoted the same approach. The state ultimately abandoned the policy too and left the task of working among the Indians to the Jesuits and other religious who had in the interim adopted a reserve approach. The religious had concluded that contact between the two races led not to the ennoblement of the Indian but rather to the debauchery of the Frenchman. Contact, that is, tended to emphasize the worst traits of both races. To avoid this, and to regulate the brandy traffic, they opted for a reserve system where Christianity, if not civilization, could be promoted. Stanley's other two articles develop these themes further.

Cornelius Jaenen also treats with this issue in "The Frenchification and Evangelization of the Amerindians in Seventeenth Century New France" [137]. This article, which is highly intellectual in its approach, suggests origins for the "frenchification" policy in "Catholic apocalypticalism" and a "cultural superiority complex" on the part of the French. He also suggests that such a policy, with assimilation as its ultimate goal, was viewed "as a means of achieving the populationist objective of the mercantilists while averting Louis XIV's fear of de-populating France through immigration" (p. 68). On the surface there appears to be here some support for Parkman's suggestion that the French "cherished" the Indian. But Jaenen quickly points out that the view of the Indian as a noble savage who should be elevated through "frenchification" and "evangelization" had a very short life-span, and, despite the precarious French tenure in Canada, "the concept of Amerindians as bloodthirsty, filthy depraved barbarians replaced the view of the natural savage" (p. 69). Two further articles by Jaenen are "Amerindian Views of French Culture in the Seventeenth Century" [139] and "Problems of As-similation in New France, 1603–1645" [136]. *Louis-bourg and the Indians: A Study in Imperial Race Relations, 1713–1760*, by Olive P. Dickason [72], contains a fine chapter concerning French Indian policy. Among the items she discusses are Champlain's dream of a mixed race and intermarriage as official policy before 1700. These are also treated by Jaenen, who reaches differ-ent conclusions in "The Meeting of the French and Amerindians in the Seventeenth Century [138].

The policy that promoted assimilation was reck-oned a failure by both the religious and civil authorities of New France before the end of the seventeenth century. Missionary work continued, however, both in the Saint Lawrence colony and in the interior. For an examination of the missionary work generally, see Father Camille de Rochemonteix, *Les Jésuites et la Nouvelle-France au dix-septième siècle d'après beaucoup de documents inédits* [200]. This three-volume work was published in 1895. In 1906 he published his two-volume study of the eighteenth century [201]. Lionel Groulx provides a general view of seventeenth-century missionary activity in "Missionnaires de l'est en Nouvelle-France" [105], and Francis J. Nelligan covers a somewhat later period in "Catholic Missionary Labours on the Lake Superior Frontier, 1667–1751" [181]. Marcel Trudel produced an exhaustive study of a little-publicized chapter of New France with his *"L'esclavage au Canada français"* [266].

In his article "The First Indian 'Reserves' in Canada" [235], George F. G. Stanley examined the origins and early development of Indian settlements at Sillery, Becancour, Lorette, Caughnawaga, Saint Regis, and Lac des Deux Montagnes (Oka). These, of course, were the locations where missionaries—Sulpicians and Jesuits—ministered to the Indians who attached themselves to their care. These included Algonquins, Hurons, Nipissings, Abenakis, and Iroquois. The last were converts to Christianity from the confederacy who sought to live among Christians and showed that not all missions to the Iroquois were failures. Two aspects of these reserves should be noted as an indicator of

French Indian policy. First, the reserves were granted to a religious order for the purpose of ministering to the Indians. The exception was Sillery, where the grant made it clear that the land was the property of the Indians. The significance lies in the granting agency. The French did not recognize any aboriginal proprietary rights in land, as the British would do in 1763. The point was not important during the French regime, for the French population was never so great as to threaten Indians in their possession of land, though it would later be significant. Abbé H.-A. Scott relates the story of Sillery in the seventeenth century in *Une paroisse historique de la Nouvelle-France: Notre Dame de Sainte-Foy, 1541–1670* [217]. See also his "La Bourgade Saint-Joseph de Sillery après 1670" [218] and "La Bourgade Saint-Joseph de Sillery après 1670: Etablissement de Saint-Françoise-de-Sales" [219]. The second point concerns the Saint Regis reserve. Begun in 1752, it was one means by which the French hoped to secure Iroquois support against the English in the war that everyone was expecting and that did come a year or two later. The Saint Regis Indians took very little part in the Seven Years War, but that mission had been established with the military motive in mind. The Saint Regis mission therefore was an overt example of the French including the Indians in their imperial aspirations. Only the location of the mission was somewhat different, for the Indians on the frontier line had, since the War of the Spanish Succession, figured in France's imperial thinking.

Concurrent with the "frenchification" program, which was pursued at best halfheartedly, the French carried on a commercial side of Indian affairs. This was related directly to the Iroquois wars. Because of the presence on the Hudson River of a rival European country—the Dutch until 1664 and the English after that date—the French could not permit the Iroquois to establish commercial relations with the Algonquin-speaking tribes of the Saint Lawrence and the Great Lakes. To do so would have opened the possibility that the furs from the north would be diverted to the Hudson River, thereby destroying the economy of New France. Yet this in turn meant that the war with the Iroquois would continue. As George T. Hunt demonstrated in *The Wars of the Iroquois* [131], the confederacy felt it needed those furs and had asserted itself against Huronia to acquire them. At the same time, though forbidden to do so by the king and the minister of marine, the French in Canada extended their fur trading westward to Fort Frontenac and into the Ohio and Mississippi valleys. This expansion required good relations with the interior tribes, whose cooperation was essential for the success of a fur trading venture. Ironically, the presence of the Iroquois assisted the French in dealings with the western tribes. Two fine studies by W. J. Eccles treat this period of the French regime particularly well: *Canada under Louis XIV, 1663–1701* [76], and *Frontenac: The Courtier Governor* [75]. Also see Emma Lewis Coleman, *New England Captives Carried to Canada* [54].

French Imperialism and the Indians

Then suddenly events turned everything around. The wars with the Iroquois ended, which gave the French some breathing space. A unique view of this settlement is Anthony F. C. Wallace, "Origins of Iroquois Neutrality: The Grand Settlement of 1701" [279]. The treaty of 1701 called for the Iroquois to remain neutral in any future Anglo-French war, and the new French policy toward the confederacy become one of maintaining that neutrality. While the peace was welcome to the French, it did create a secondary problem. The Iroquois had been weakened by the long war and were disinclined to fight the western tribes to prevent them from bringing their furs across Iroquois territory to Albany. And in the first decade of the eighteenth century, many began to do so. In this fashion the French found their commercial relations with the western tribes threatened.

This happened at an awkward time, for France's attitude toward North America changed totally on the eve of the War of the Spanish Succession in Europe. Louis XIV now decided to strengthen his position in America, and to do so he ordered the establishment of a French colony at the mouth of the Mississippi, with military posts to be established from there to the Great Lakes, in order to confine the English to their coastal colonies. As W. J. Eccles writes in *The Canadian Frontier 1534–1760* [77]: "This was imperialism with a vengeance. A handful of French officers, fur traders and priests were to hold the allegiance of the western nations and seek to retain possession of most of North America—this at a time when traders from the English colonies were beginning to move into the trans-Allegheny west" (p. 130).

From this point until the conquest and retention of Canada by the British in 1760 and 1763, French policy toward the Indians was dictated by imperial considerations. The fur trading did not stop, nor did the missionary activity. But both were included in the general imperial design to retain the French empire in North America, and that meant retaining control of the Mississippi Valley and the Ohio Valley. And that, in turn, meant securing the friendship and military assistance of the interior Indian tribes. Images of the Indian as noble savage or worthless barbarian were pushed into the background, and the image of the Indian as warrior became dominant (see Surtees [247]).

Three excellent articles in the *Canadian Historical Review* by Yves F. Zoltvany are the best entrances to the French western policy in the early eighteenth century: "New France and the West, 1701–1713" [291]; "The Frontier Policy of Philippe Rigaud de Vaudreuil, 1713–1725" [292]; and "The Problem of Western Policy under Philippe de Rigaud de Vaudreuil (1703–1725)" [290]. Zoltvany has also written a biography, *Philippe de Rigaud de Vaudreuil: Governor of New France, 1703–1725* [293]. Marcel Giraud, *Le métis canadien: Son rôle dans l'histoire des provinces de l'ouest* [94], is a monumental work and should be consulted concerning French relations with the western interior Indians.

In their efforts to secure Indian allies the French adopted some highly successful, and highly expensive, devices. The use of king's posts assisted in keeping prices competitive with those of the English traders; the endorsement of the coureurs de bois, hitherto regarded as renegades, assisted crown policy; the founding of Detroit, though costly, actually hurt the French; the lavish distribution of gifts was an effective method of diplomacy, one also used by the British. On the whole, the French were able to retain their hegemony over the interior. For a good study of one aspect of this policy see Wilbur R. Jacobs, *Wilderness Politics and Indian Gifts: The Northern Colonial Frontier, 1748–1763* [135]. The most succinct and authoritative account of the imperial period of French policy is W. J. Eccles, *The Canadian Frontier* [77]. This volume concerns itself with more than Indian policy, of course, but it is one of the few works that integrate Indian relations into the general context of the period.

The imperial policy of France finally failed during the Seven Years War, and Britain, when it conquered Canada in 1760, determined to keep it after the peace treaty. A good account of the war can be found in Eccles, *The Canadian Frontier* [77], and in George F. G. Stanley, *New France: The Last Phase, 1744–1760* [243]. The period of the war is also covered in Jacobs, *Wilderness Politics and Indian Gifts* [135].

Acadia

The French policy toward the Indians of Acadia was based on the same general principles and sentiments as their policy in the rest of New France, but the emphasis was somewhat different. The role of Acadia in the general scheme of French North America is outlined in W. J. Eccles's *The Canadian Frontier* [77]. Note should also be taken of Wilson D. and Ruth S. Wallis, *The Micmac Indians of Eastern Canada* [280], and Andrew H. Clark, *Acadia: The Geography of Early Nova Scotia to 1760* [50].

In this theater the military aspects of Indian policy seemed to be predominant, and here as well the French were more successful than the English in securing the loyalty of the Micmacs and the neighboring tribes. As elsewhere the gift-giving, the awarding of medals, the trade and the missionary work were all integrated into the French treatment of the Indians. For their part, the Indians grew dependent on French trade goods, and they also accepted Christianity—with modifications. They were quite prepared to fight the English from the New England colonies and, after 1714, from Nova Scotia. Indeed, they remained steadfast in their loyalty to the French even after Acadia "with the ancient boundaries" was ceded to Britain. They were, in fact, a principal reason the British were unable to establish effective control over Acadia until after 1760. They adopted this stance largely for self-interest, to retain their lands, which were more secure while the French were present to counterbalance the English threat. The unique nature of the missionaries in Acadia, however, no doubt also encouraged this stance. They would accompany, and lead, war parties and generally promoted actions against the English when they could. Most studies make it clear that the Micmac attachment to the French resulted to a large degree from self-interest, but the extent and loyalty of that attachment was undoubtedly increased by the policy of the French and the activity of the priests, some of whom co-opted shamans in northern Algonquin societies in their efforts at missionization, a subject analyzed by Robert Conkling in "Legitimacy and Conversion in Social Change: The Case of the French Missionaries and the Northeastern Algonkian" [55].

Richard V. Bannon has described the labors of a missionary in "Antoine Gaulin, 1674—1770: An Apostle of Early Acadie" [9], and Albert David has examined the career of perhaps the most effective of the missionaries in two articles, "Messire Pierre Maillard, apôtre des Micmacs" [68], and "L'apôtre des Micmacs" [69]. A protégé of Maillard, and without doubt the most notorious of the French priests in Acadia, "The Abbé Le Loutre" [204] was the subject of a fascinating article by Norman McL. Rogers in the 1930 *Canadian Historical Review*. Micheline Dumont Johnson has contributed a biography of Maillard to the *Dictionary of Canadian Biography* [145] and has also written a book about the role of missionaries in eighteenth-century Acadia entitled, appropriately, *Apôtres ou agitateurs* [144]. Lucien Campeau's *La première mission d'Acadie* [21] is also recommended. Pierre Belliveau's "Indians and Some Raids on Massachusetts about 1690–1704" [12] discusses warfare during King William's War, and a study prepared for National Historical Parks and

Sites by Olive P. Dickason, *Louisbourg and the Indians* [72], gives an account for the Micmac resistance to the British. Two older works also bear mentioning: D. C. Harvey, *The French Régime in Prince Edward Island* [111], and "Lettre de M. l'Abbé Maillard" [173]. E. Palmer Patterson's general study *The Canadian Indian: A History since 1500* [183] contains a brief summary of the French policy, and Leslie F. S. Upton, though concerned primarily with the British regime, does deliver a succinct account of French-Indian-British relations from 1700 to 1760 in his *Micmacs and Colonists* [274], which supersedes his earlier article, "Colonists and Micmacs" [269].

The British Period: 1763–1867

Introduction

After the conquest and the 1763 Treaty of Paris, Britain retained Canada and became the only European power to have official contact with the Indians of the northeastern woodlands. The policy Britain adopted, through the Royal Proclamation of that year, was quite simply one of avoiding, or at least minimizing, contact with the Indians in order to reduce conflicts.

That all-embracing document established the general colonial philosophy of the British government for North America. It also provided the first constitution for the newly-acquired colony of Canada, and it set forth rules of behavior for British subjects toward the Indians. Clarence Alvord, in "The Genesis of the Proclamation of 1763" [5], argued that a desire to quiet the Indians prompted the document, especially in light of the Pontiac War, which is best discussed by Howard H. Peckham in *Pontiac and the Indian Uprising* [186]. Others have argued that the news of the Pontiac War did not reach England in time to influence the policymakers. The second edition of *Native Rights in Canada* [64] asserts that, Pontiac notwithstanding, the document confirmed and clarified Indian rights that had existed for at least the previous decade.

Regardless of its origins, the Royal Proclamation created a huge Indian reserve bounded, approximately, by the Mississippi River, the Appalachian highlands, and a line drawn from the south shore of Lake Nipissing, in Ontario, to cross the Saint Lawrence River at forty five degrees north latitude. The bulk of this territory lay within the confines of what would become the United States, but it also included what would become southern Ontario. Also it should be noted that, in Canada, the lands to the east of the Lake Nipissing line were not included in the reserve. Within the reserve, Indians were recognized as proprietors; non-Indians were forbidden to move into it, and any who were already there were ordered to remove themselves. Lands could be purchased, but only by the crown; and non-Indians could enter the reserve to trade, but only by license and at garrisoned posts.

The task of administering this policy was given to

the Indian Department that had been created in 1755. The story of the creation of the Indian Branch can be found in John R. Alden, "The Albany Congress and the Creation of the Indian Superintendencies" [2], and in Robert S. Allen, *The British Indian Department and the Frontier in North America: 1755–1830* [4]. The branch had been formed to help secure Indian support against the French. The previous system of permitting each colony to administer its own Indian affairs had been found wanting, and the imperial government decided to assume that responsibility. A brief account of this transformation, and of the career of Sir William Johnson, who assumed charge of the northern superintendency, can be found in Wilbur R. Jacobs, *Wilderness Politics and Indian Gifts* [135]. The story of Sir William and the origins of the branch lies within the history of the United States, of course. It is mentioned here, however, because it was this branch that extended its sway to include Canada after the Seven Years War. Although the French menace had been removed on the northern frontier after 1763, the branch remained in existence to administer the Indian country and the fur trade.

The policy outlined in the royal proclamation continued for twenty years. Beginning in 1774, however, the Indian Branch was called upon to reembrace the original cause of its existence. Indian support was to be curried again, not to protect the empire against the French, but to assist in suppressing the rebellious American colonists. Barbara Graymont has recounted their role in *The Iroquois in the American Revolution* [103], as has George F. G. Stanley in "The Six Nations and the American Revolution" [242]. Other aspects of the policy of using Indians in the Revolutionary War have been examined in S. F. Wise, "The American Revolution and Indian History" [288]; Nelson V. Russell, "The Indian Policy of Henry Hamilton" [213]; and G. E. Raeman, *The Trail of the Iroquois Indians: How the Iroquois Nation Saved Canada for the British Empire* [194]. An overview can be found also in Robert S. Allen [4] and in George F. G. Stanley's *Canada's Soldiers* [240], and Jack M. Sosin discussed the issue in his 1965 article "The Use of Indians in the War of the American Revolution: A Re-assessment of Responsibility" [232]. Sosin's *Whitehall and the Wilderness* [231] also provides a good survey of Indian relations for the 1760 to 1775 period.

Land Policy

The success of the Revolution created a crisis in Canada. Loyalist refugees from the American colonies had to be settled, and the Indians who had served Britain well on the northern frontier, especially the Six Nations, were angry with the terms of the peace treaty and had to be placated. British response to the crisis involved a modification of British Indian policy. Governor Haldimand, in Quebec, authorized the acquisition of land from the Canadian Iroquois and from the Mississaugas north of lakes Erie and Ontario. The purpose was to settle the Loyalists west of the Ottawa River and to provide land for the Six Nations and other allied Indians who might choose to take up residence in Canada in compensation for lands lost in the United States. Haldimand's action meant a de facto abandonment of the policy of the Indian reserve, for the Mississauga lands clearly lay within the bounds of the proclamation region. The circumstances surrounding Haldimand's vital decision are discussed, albeit briefly, in Gerald M. Craig, *Upper Canada: The Formative Years, 1784–1841* (chap. 1) [57], and in Lillian F. Gates, *Land Policies of Upper Canada* (chaps. 1 and 2) [91].

Over the next half-century a series of land surrenders acquired for the crown the entire region of southern Ontario from the bands who occupied it in 1783. Policy clearly changed from protecting the Indians from White encroachments on their land to purchasing land through the crown for settlement and, to a lesser extent, for military purposes. The most complete study of these land cessions to date is one prepared in 1943 by J. L. Morris, with the somewhat misleading title *Indians of Ontario* [177]. This study, reprinted in 1964, includes a large map outlining the several surrenders. It should be used in conjunction with the collection known as *Indian Treaties and Surrenders from 1680 to 1890*, published in 1891 in two volumes by the Queen's Printer, and reissued in 1973 in three volumes by the Coles Publishing Company [22].

An earlier study by Gilbert C. Paterson, *Land Set-*

tlement in Upper Canada, 1783–1840 [182], includes a chapter and a map concerning Indian lands, but it is rather incomplete and must be used with extreme caution. E. A. Cruickshank has edited the papers of Lieutenant Governor John Graves Simcoe [62] and his successor, Peter Russell [63], for publication by the Ontario Historical Society, and these two sets provide an enormous amount of data concerning Indian lands, and Indian policy in general, for the first decade of Upper Canada's history. This correspondence also demonstrates how vital the issue of Indian affairs was in the early years of the province of Ontario.

Two groups of Six Nations Indians, largely Mohawks, availed themselves of Haldimand's offer to provide land in Canada. C. H. Torok's "The Tyendinaga Mohawks" [257] and M. Eleanor Herrington's "Captain John Deserontyou and the Mohawk Settlement at Deseronto" [120], as well as E. A. Cruickshank's "The Coming of the Loyalist Mohawks to the Bay of Quinté" [60], examine the origins of the settlement established in the region of the Bay of Quinté in 1784. Charles M. Johnston's *The Valley of the Six Nations* [147] remains the best single source concerning the band that followed Joseph Brant into Canada to settle at the Grand River. Brant also caused some discomfort for Canadian officials regarding those lands. Because his group had received its land by patent, and not under the general terms of the royal proclamation, Brant claimed that they could sell or lease those lands without resorting to the mediation of the crown; and in general he claimed a type of separate status for the Indian loyalists. This aspect of Indian land policy, and the importance of Indians in the early years of Upper Canada, are discussed in E. G. Firth's "The Administration of Peter Russell, 1796–1799" [83] and in Charles M. Johnston's "Joseph Brant, the Grand River Lands, and the Northwest Crisis" [146]. Johnston's article concerning "William Claus and John Norton" [148] treats with an interesting quarrel that grew out of the Six Nations enclave on the Grand River.

Military Policy

Haldimand shaped more than land policy, however. Faced with the crisis of incoming Loyalist refugees and angry Indians in 1783, he took two further steps. He encouraged the generous distribution of gifts among the Indians. In this, of course, he was simply continuing the policy described in Jacobs's *Wilderness Politics and Indian Gifts* [135], but it was extended to include Indians outside British territory, and it would continue until 1858. See James A. Clifton's manuscript on this topic, "'Visiting Indians' in Canada" [53]. Also, as A. L. Burt argues in "A New Approach to the Problem of the Western Posts" [18], Haldimand's fear of the Indians caused him to retain possession of the western posts, including Niagara, Detroit, Sandusky, and Michilimackinac, though these lay within the boundaries of the United States. See also A. L. Burt's *The*

United States, Great Britain and British North America [19] and G. S. Graham, "The Indian Menace and the Retention of the Western Posts" [100]. This decision created a central issue in Canadian-American relations until 1796, when Britain finally handed over the posts according to the terms of the Jay Treaty. In that thirteen-year period, however, it added a new dimension to British Indian policy, for it meant that Britain, by her continued presence in United States territory, became involved—directly and deliberately said the Americans, inadvertently said the British—in the Indian-American conflict in the Ohio Valley. A series of studies has treated this issue and this period.

Reginald Horsman's biography *Matthew Elliott: British Indian Agent* [126] examines Elliott and the British Indian Department's activities and policy to the War of 1812, and his *The Frontier in the Formative Years, 1783–1815* [128] also contains a description of the Indian policy of Britain and the United States in a wider context. His "The British Indian Department and the Abortive Treaty of Lower Sandusky, 1793" [124] is a very good account of that council, which led directly to Wayne's invasion of the Ohio country, an event Horsman discusses in "The British Indian Department and the Resistance to General Anthony Wayne, 1793–1795" [125]. Indian successes in 1790 and 1791 in the Old Northwest gave encouragement to the British in Canada and briefly caused them to think in terms of creating an Indian buffer state in the Ohio country. This is the topic examined by Orpha Leavitt, "British

Policy on the Canadian Frontier, 1782–92: Mediation and an Indian Buffer State" [158], and by S. F. Wise "The Indian Diplomacy of John Graves Simcoe" [287]. See also James Clifton's "Merchant, Soldier, Broker, Chief: A Corrected Obituary of Captain Billy Caldwell" [52].

From these studies, British Indian policy in the period 1783–96 emerges as one in which the Indians were encouraged to consider the British as friends. But agents were given express orders to avoid making a commitment to assist the Indians in a military sense against the United States. It was a deceptive policy. It caused consternation among the Indians, who naturally expected from the British more tangible support than presents and promises of friendship. And it angered the Americans, who resented the British presence in the western posts and suspected British motives in distributing presents. The policy suffered badly after Wayne's victory at Fallen Timbers and after the Jay Treaty secured the British retreat from the western posts.

Yet that same policy continued after 1796. The gift-giving continued; the British garrisons were relocated at Saint Joseph, Malden, and Niagara, and agents were told to continue to seek Indian friendship. But Indian policy also declined in importance in the decade after 1796 as Anglo-American relations improved, with the result that the activities of the Indian Branch in the west came less and less to the attention of the lieutenant governor or the Executive Council of Upper

Canada. In that decade, the chief concern regarding Indians was the execution of the policy of securing Indian lands.

But this *First Rapprochement* between Britain and the United States (as described by Bradford Perkins [187]) came to a sudden end as the maritime quarrels between the two countries increased in intensity during the Napoleonic blockade. E. A. Cruickshank has discussed the impact of this quarrel on Upper Canada and on Indian policy in a long article, "The 'Chesapeake' Crisis as It Affected Upper Canada" [59], which describes the revitalization of the department as the possibility of war grew. Reginald Horsman has also contributed an article, "British Indian Policy in the Northwest, 1807–1812" [123], and a book, *Expansion and American Indian Policy, 1783–1812* [127].

The war did come, of course, and British policy at that point was simply to secure whatever support could be had from the Indians of Canada itself or from potential allies in the United States, where Tecumseh and the western Indians had already taken up arms against the Americans. It was easy to secure the active assistance of the western Indians, for they had their own reasons for fighting and were eager for the British to provide them with assistance and weapons. It was more difficult to convince Indians resident in Canada to take up arms. The story of this effort and its relative success is the subject of E. A. Cruickshank's "The Employment of Indians in the War of 1812" [58] and two articles by George F. G. Stanley, "The Indians in the

War of 1812" [236] and "The Significance of the Six Nations' Participation in the War of 1812" [241]. Accounts of events in the war written by certain officers of the Indian Department can be found in E. A. Cruickshank, ed., "Campaigns of 1812–14: Contemporary Narratives by Captain W. H. Merritt, Colonel William Claus, Lieut.-Colonel Matthew Elliott, and Captain John Norton" [61], and in Carl F. Klinck and James J. Talman, eds., *The Journal of Major John Norton, 1816* [151]. Overviews of the war that are attentive to Indian participation and British policy in promoting Indian activity include Alec R. Gilpin, *The War of 1812 in the Old Northwest* [93], and John K. Mahon, *The War of 1812* [172].

The Reserve Policy

Although the military aspect of British Indian policy continued in the postwar years, it gave way to other considerations. A larger White population, increased through immigration, reduced the value of Indians as a military asset, especially as the threat of hostilities with the United States receded. Concurrently, pressures were exerted on government to secure more lands from the Indians for settlement. The policy of treating for Indian lands was therefore accelerated, and unlike the prewar years, less concern had to be given toward Indian sentiments. In the official mind, as well as in the public view, Indians were seen less as warriors or potential warriors and increasingly as a barrier to progress, or even as a nuisance (Robert J. Surtees, "The Changing Image of the Canadian Indian" [247]).

Not everyone accepted the view of the Indians as a nuisance. Missionaries, largely Protestant, but some Catholic, had begun to preach among the bands of Upper Canada and had had some success in promoting a settled and Christian life. Leslie R. Gray's "The Moravian Missionaries, Their Indians, and the Canadian Government" [102] outlines the story of the Moravian mission on the Thames River, begun in 1792. More complete is the combined work of Elma E. Gray and Leslie R. Gray, *Wilderness Christians: The Moravian Mission to the Delaware Indians* [101]. The Moravians, of course, were immigrants from the United States. Another aspect of the passage across the international border is found in James A. Clifton, *A Place of Refuge for All Time: Migration of the American Potawatomi into Upper Canada, 1830 to 1850* [51]. For other accounts of this missionary activity, its philosophy and its effect on Indian policy, one should consult Jean Usher, "Apostles and Aborigines: The Social Theory of the Church Missionary Society" [275]. Two very old accounts, which are still useful partly because they are themselves historical documents, are Alvin Torry, *Autobiography of Rev. Alvin Torry, First Missionary to the Six Nations and the Northwestern Tribes of British North America* [258], and Benjamin Slight, *Indian Researches* [226]. Peter Jones's journal, *Life and Journals of Kah-Ke-Wa-Quo-Na-By (Rev. Peter Jones)* [149], is an almost indispensable source. Also good is Fred Landon, ed., "Selections from the Papers of James Evans, Missionary to the Indians" [153], as is Charles M. Johnston, *The Valley of the Six Nations* [147]. An Indian perspective can be found in Van Dusen's *The Indian Chief* [277].

The British government was influenced at this time by evangelical organizations that were pressing for better treatment of native peoples throughout the empire. G. R. Mellor's *British Imperial Trusteeship* [174] and Grenfell Price's *White Settlers and Native Peoples* [190] treat this factor, including its application in North America. American influence also affected policy in Canada. The United States had already adopted a program of promoting civilization and settlement, and many of the Methodists working among the Indians were American in origin or training. This worried Canadian officials, who were highly suspect of American democracy. Lieutenant Governor Maitland, for example, advised that Indians be taught civilization by British missionaries, who would promote British, not republican, values, and he began a private project among the Credit River Mississaugas to promote that end. It proved successful enough to encourage both Maitland and other officials.

These several factors—a changing image of the Indians, missionary activity, imperial considerations, and suspicions of the Americans—combined to cause the adoption of a new policy toward Indians in Canada. Two articles discuss this process: Leslie F. S. Upton, "The Origins of Canadian Indian Policy" [267], and Robert J. Surtees, "The Development of an Indian Reserve Policy in Canada" [245]. The new policy, adopted officially in 1830, was intended to promote the civilization and Christianization of the Indians. To do that, the government intended to collect the Indians on reserved lands. There they would be ministered to by missionaries, taught by teachers, and trained by tradesmen and farmers. In addition, houses were to be built for them, and other assistance, such as agricultural implements, was to be provided. It was at this time also that the policy of commuting the annual presents to tools and other implements was begun. It was expected that these influences would convince the Indians to accept Christianity and generally to adopt a settled and "civilized" way of life. It was also expected that progress on the reserves would be great enough to incline the nomadic Indians to settle on reserves of their own. Such assimilation, if successful, would theoretically end the need for both reserves and the Indian Branch, which was given the task of implementing the new policy, for the Indians would become capable of coping with and participating in White society. This would remain the policy of the British until they turned Indian affairs over to Canadian jurisdiction in 1860. The 1830 change also saw the final transfer of the department from military to civil control. Each reserve was placed under the control of a resident agent who reported to the chief superintendent, who in turn reported to the lieutenant governor.

The program was instituted with two experiments

in 1830, at Coldwater on Lake Simcoe and on the Saint
Clair River. Other reserves were set aside over the
years. In some cases bands were granted parcels of
land in areas where they had already sold their rights.
Examples are Coldwater and Rice Lake. Other reserve
villages were begun on land reserved in previous
treaties. Future treaties invariably provided land for
reserves as a matter of policy.

Two major government reports provide the best
descriptions of the application of the policy in the years
following 1830. The first, the *Report on the Affairs of the
Indians in Canada*, was published in two installments in
the appendixes of the Journals of the Legislative Assembly of Canada (Appendix EEE for 1844–45 and
Appendix T for 1847) [40] [41]. The second, *Report of
the Special Commissioners to Investigate Indian Affairs in
Canada*, was printed as Appendix 21 of the 1858 Sessional Papers [42]. A more concise account of the administration of the period is a chapter entitled "Indian
Affairs: The White Man's Albatross" in J. E. Hodgetts,
Pioneer Public Service [121]. Duncan C. Scott, a former
deputy minister of Indian affairs, provided *The Administration of Indian Affairs in Canada* [223] and wrote
short summaries of Indian affairs in the multivolume
history *Canada and Its Provinces*, edited by Adam Shortt
and A. G. Doughty [220, 221, 222]. These are dated,
however, and somewhat superficial. Some insight into
the Manitoulin Island experiment can be gained from
Rundell M. Lewis, "The Manitoulin Letters of Rev.
Charles Crosbie Brough" [162]; and the "Anderson

Record" [212] by S. Rowe recounts the career of T. G. Anderson, who was placed in charge of the Coldwater reserve in 1830 and the Manitoulin Island establishment in 1836, and who ultimately became chief superintendent of Indian affairs. Ruth Bleasdale also centered on the Manitoulin case in her "Manitowaning: An Experiment in Indian Settlement" [14], and Douglas Leighton has written an account, "The Manitoulin Incident of 1863: An Indian-White Confrontation in the Province of Canada" [160]. Elizabeth Graham has produced a fine little book, *Medicine Man to Missionary: Missionaries as Agents for Change among the Indians of Southern Ontario, 1784–1867* [99], and Donald J. Wilson discusses the question of Indian education in "'No Blanket to Be Worn in School': The Education of Indians in Early Nineteenth Century Ontario" [286]. Peter S. Schmalz's *The History of the Saugeen Indians* [216] provides a good demonstration of how the reserve policy and the continuing treaty surrender process affected one group of Indians on the Saugeen peninsula. Edward S. Rogers has published numerous studies concerning the Indians of Canada. Particular attention is directed here to "Parry Island Farmers: A Period of Change in the Way of Life of the Algonkians of Southern Ontario" [203], which he and Flora Tobobondung prepared in 1975.

These several studies reveal that officials of the Indian Branch encountered a variety of problems regarding the new policy. These included the continued encroachments by Whites on Indian lands, challenges by Whites to the agent's authority, desires for more land, the sale of liquor on reserves, Indian resistance to the civilization program, and the question of landownership on reserves. Regarding the last, there were those who advocated the use of individual title deeds, in fee simple, on the grounds that pride in ownership would accelerate the civilization process. Opponents argued that title deeds would quickly pass into White hands, through sale or chicanery, thereby depriving the Indians of even the small parcels of lands they retained, and in the process destroying the reserves where the program of civilization was to take place. This controversy played itself out in the 1830s. Deeds were not granted; rather, other systems of landownership on reserves were devised, and these are explained in William B. Henderson, *Canada's Indian Reserves: Pre-Confederation* [117].

Obviously the agents were forced to become concerned with protecting the Indians from Whites as well as with civilizing them for entry into White society. This theme is expanded in John L. Tobias's fine article, "Protection, Civilization, Assimilation: An Outline History of Canada's Indian Policy" [252]. Tobias also points out differences between the reserves of Upper Canada and those of Lower Canada in the pre-Confederation nineteenth century. Donald Smith's *Le Sauvage* [230] explains the background to that difference, which is also revealed in the *Report on the Affairs of the Indians in Canada* [40–42]. Despite the poor grades accorded by commentators and observers of the day to the policy of civilization and Christianization by means of reserves, there was never any suggestion of abandoning it. Rather it was reinforced with legislation designed to protect the Indians. Likewise, concurrent legislation provided a means for Indians to lose (actually to reject) that protection once they had progressed sufficiently in civilized ways to become full citizens. This process by which an Indian ceased legally to be an Indian became known as enfranchisement and remains a part of Indian policy to the present. The pre-Confederation legislation concerning protection and enfranchisement is discussed in the first section of *The Historical Development of the Indian Act* [161], edited by John Leslie and Ron Maguire of the Research Branch of the Department of Indian and Northern Affairs. That branch, currently directed by Dr. Katie Cooke, has been very active in preparing specialized studies concerning Indian affairs. Another of these is Henderson's study *Canada's Indian Reserves: Pre-Confederation* [117], already mentioned, which examines the way reserves were set aside before 1867. It deals not only with the reserves in the two Canadas, but also with those in Nova Scotia, New Brunswick, and Prince Edward Island, all of which had become part of British North America with the cession of Acadia to Britain by the French after the Seven Years War.

The Maritime Colonies

The cession of Acadia, and the prior expulsion of the Acadians in 1755, eliminated the French influence from the region and brought the Micmacs and their neighbors squarely into a confrontation with the British. Previously the British had had little success in securing Indian support in the Atlantic region, despite their best efforts. These efforts have been examined in two articles by R. O. MacFarlane, "British Indian Policy in Nova Scotia to 1760" [168] and "Indian Trade in Nova Scotia to 1764" [167]; and a unique aspect of British efforts was uncovered by J. B. Brebner, ed., "Subsidized Intermarriage with the Indians: An Incident in British Colonial Policy" [16].

After 1763 the Indian affairs of Acadia (Nova Scotia) were integrated into the general North American British Indian administration. This transition is dealt with in Elizabeth Ann Hutton, "Indian Affairs in Nova Scotia 1760–1834" [133], and in Leslie F. S. Upton, *Micmacs and Colonists: Indian-White Relations in the Maritimes, 1713–1867* [274]. The British attitude toward the Indians in the Maritimes differed, however, from their views of the Indians of the Canadas. In the latter there had been a tradition of friendship and loyalty with the Six Nations, and later with the western Indians. Furthermore, the terms of the surrender of Montreal in 1760 had secured the Indians in their possessions and freedoms. This was not the case in the Maritimes, where the Micmacs had resisted the British till the end. Nor was there a proclamation line to protect Indian lands. Reserves were ultimately set apart, but these were often infringed upon and were designed to remove Indians to isolated locations. Settlers and colonists resented the Indians' presence either because they occupied desired lands or because they were considered an embarrassment. Furthermore, after the American Revolution Nova Scotia was divided into Nova Scotia and New Brunswick, and later Prince Edward Island became a separate colony as well. The partitions meant that the Indians had to deal with three separate legislatures.

For Indian policy in the period from 1760 to the beginnings of Canadian control at Confederation in 1867, the extensive work of Leslie F. S. Upton is the best resource. His recent book *Micmacs and Colonists* [274], released shortly before his untimely death, is a fine study of the period of British control. But his earlier work, in the form of scholarly articles, should also be consulted. His "Colonists and Micmacs" [269] outlines the colonists' attitudes toward the Indians, including the view that the Indians were an embarrassment when potential settlers for the colony were sought. Three articles in *Acadiensis* deal with Indian affairs and policies in each of the Maritime colonies: "Indian Affairs in Colonial New Brunswick" [268]; "Indian Policy in Colonial Nova Scotia, 1783–1871" [270]; and "Indians and Islanders: The Micmacs in Colonial Prince Edward Island" [271]. Two articles by Judith Fingard examine missionary work in the early nineteenth century: "English Humanitarianism and the Colonial Mind: Walter Bromley in Nova Scotia, 1813–1825" [82] and "The New England Company and the New Brunswick Indians, 1786–1826: A Comment on the Colonial Perversion of British Benevolence" [81].

Wayne Daugherty's *Maritime Indian Treaties in Historical Perspective* [66] examines the various peace and friendship agreements between the British and the Indians in the seventeenth and eighteenth centuries.

H. F. McGee has edited a book of readings, *The Native Peoples of Atlantic Canada: A History of Ethnic Interaction* [169], that contains several items concerning policy in the Maritimes. It also contains two extracts from James P. Howley, *The Beothuks or Red Indians: The Aboriginal Inhabitants of Newfoundland* [129]. The most recent title concerning this tragic episode of Indian history in Canada is Frederick W. Rowe, *Extinction: The Beothuks of Newfoundland* [211]. It is a good work that attempts to dispel the many myths concerning the Beothuks, especially the charge of deliberate genocide. Upton also dealt with this question in "The Extermination of the Beothuks of Newfoundland" [272] and "The Beothuks: Questions and Answers" [273].

The Canadian Period: 1867 to the Present

Introduction

The British government transferred control of Indian affairs to the province of Canada in 1860. With the achievement of Confederation in 1867, "Indians and lands reserved for Indians" were placed in the list of legislative powers and responsibilities secured to the federal government by the British North America Act of 1867, section 91 (24). The immediate effect was

CANADIAN INDIAN TREATIES
AND LAND CONVEYANCES

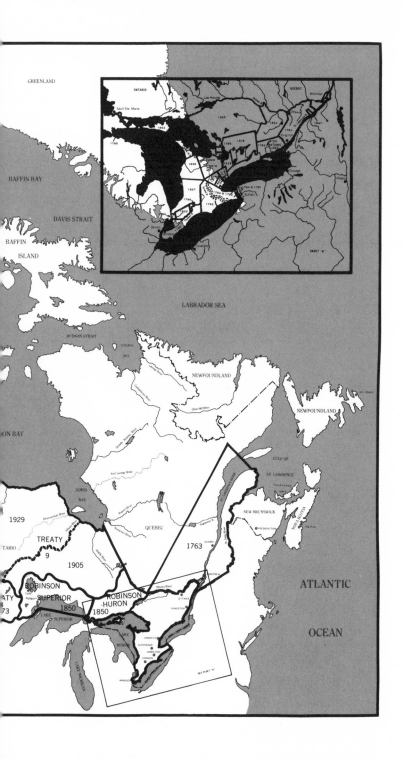

simply administrative, for the four original provinces of Ontario, Quebec, New Brunswick, and Nova Scotia (joined by Prince Edward Island in 1973) merely continued the reserve policies in place at the time. The administrative centralization of Indian affairs was confirmed with the passage, in 1868, of the first federal Indian Act.

The general framework of federal Indian policy was inherited, therefore, from the pre-Confederation period. The principles of protection and assimilation remained. The instruments of education, Christianization, and reservations were also retained. And the administrative machinery, the Indian Department, was centralized in the federal government. The policy, and its application, continued to evolve and be refined. It became increasingly legalistic in its orientation. Emphasis was directed toward enfranchisement, toward the meaning of Indian status, and toward eradicating all remnants, aspects, or symbols of tribal background or Indian heritage. The imposition of elected local governments on reserves and the proscription by federal statute of such customs as the Sun Dance and the potlatch were instances of the latter emphasis. And to promote the program, extended powers were accorded the Indian agents through an increase in the authority of the chief superintendent, who, after Confederation, was a minister of the federal government.

Canada itself evolved into a transcontinental state, thereby requiring an Indian policy that could accommodate the tribes of the prairies and the Pacific coast.

The approach, therefore, differed somewhat in different parts of the country, until in 1951 the government of Canada instituted a revised Indian Act for general application throughout the dominion.

Federal policy, with particular emphasis on the evolving Indian Act, is the central theme of John Tobias's "Protection, Civilization, Assimilation" [252], which provides the most direct introduction to the study of the Indian policy since Confederation. *The Historical Development of the Indian Act* [161], edited by John Leslie and Ron Maguire, is another good survey of the legislation and its attendant application. *Native Rights in Canada* [64] concentrates on legal questions and land rights throughout Canada. Richard H. Bartlett's "The Indian Act of Canada" [10] is an excellent summary focusing on the legal history of the act. These fairly recent studies can be supplemented by two publications of the Department of Indian Affairs and Northern Development: *Indian Status* [36], and *History of Indian Policy* [34].

The third of Duncan C. Scott's summary articles for *Canada and Its Provinces* is entitled "Indian Affairs, 1867–1912" [222]. A highly laudatory account, *The Administration of Indian Affairs in Canada* [1], was published in 1915 by Frederick H. Abbott, the secretary of the Board of Indian Commissioners in the United States. Abbott was particularly impressed with the authority and discretionary power accorded the chief superintendent and his agents in Canada, a condition he wanted to prevail in the United States also. These very powers, incidentally, were roundly condemned by Harold Cardinal in *The Unjust Society* [46].

Interest in Indian affairs appears, from published sources, to have been slight in the first half of the twentieth century, even though important treaties were negotiated in that period and vital policy decisions were made. Indian affairs remained very much a peripheral interest to Canadians and Canadian scholars. As is suggested by recent articles such as E. Palmer Patterson II, "Andrew Paull (1890–1959): Finding a Voice for the New Indian" [184], this was occasioned at least to some degree by the severe difficulties under which Indian leaders had to labor even to make grievances known. In the years following World War II, however, interest in Indian affairs was high, largely as a result of the contributions made by Indians during the war (see Tobias [252], p. 24). This interest sparked the major revisions of the Indian Act in 1951, and it also inspired a series of articles concerning Canada's Indian policy.

Allan Harper wrote three of these articles for *America Indigena*. "Canada's Indian Administration: Basic Concepts and Objectives" [108] examined the reservation system by which Indians were to be taught to work and to progress and ultimately to acquire full citizenship. His second article, "Canada's Indian Administration: The Indian Act" [109], provided an explanation of the 1927 act and described the road to full citizenship through assimilation as being a long one. "Canada's Indian Administration: The Treaty System" [110] argued that Canada's system had been superior to that of the United States. All three can be viewed as defenses of Canada's policy and its application. Two articles in the 1946 *Canadian Journal of Economics and Political Science* also were concerned with defending the policy: W. W. Beatty, "The Goal of Indian Assimilation" [11], and T. R. L. MacInnes, "History of Indian Administration in Canada" [170]. A somewhat different stance was taken by C. T. Loram and T. F. McIlwraith, eds., *The North American Indian Today* [164], which was published in 1943 and constituted proceedings of a joint Yale–University of Toronto Conference held in 1939. That conference, however, still accepted the need to civilize and Christianize the Indians, a task in which the scientist and the missionary should cooperate. For a survey of the legislative aspect of Indian policy for the long period from Confederation until the 1951 Indian Act, consult a recent report prepared for the Research Branch of the Department of Indian Affairs by Wayne Daugherty and Dennis Madill, entitled *Indian Government under Indian Act Legislation, 1868–1951* [67].

Western Canada

When Canada first acquired the lands of the Hudson's Bay Company, the Indians of the prairies had had dealings with that company and its predecessors for more than two centuries. The relationship had been largely commercial, and company policy toward the Indians had been designed to promote and ease that commerce. Arthur S. Morton's *A History of the Canadian West to 1870–71* [178] and E. E. Rich's *The History of the Hudson's Bay Company, 1670–1870*, 3 vols. [198], are excellent studies of the period before Canada acquired the West. Arthur J. Ray and Donald B. Freeman have written *"Give Us Good Measure": An Economic Analysis of Relations between the Indians and the Hudson's Bay Company before 1763* [197], and Arthur J. Ray has added *Indians in the Fur Trade* [195].

The first task of the Canadian government in the West was the acquisition of Indian lands for settlement and for the construction of a transcontinental railway. The method chosen to secure that land was the treaty system, which had worked well in Ontario. Between 1871 and 1877, seven major land cessions secured the southern and central portion of the Canadian West for the government. *The Birth of Western Canada* by George F. G. Stanley [239] is perhaps the best introduction to the Canadian government's first entry into the West and to its first efforts to apply the land treaty and reserve systems there. Stanley's prime concern in discussing these matters, however, was to attempt to explain the armed rebellion that occurred in the West in 1885. This early period of western Canadian history has received considerable attention.

In 1880 Alexander Morris, who had been a principal negotiator for the government at four of the treaties, published *The Treaties of Canada with the Indians of Manitoba and the North-West Territories* [176]. His account was contradicted slightly by John McDougall's

Opening the Great West [166] regarding Treaty Six. Another good description of Treaty Six is that by Peter Erasmus in *Buffalo Days and Nights* [79]. Erasmus was the interpreter at the proceedings that led to the treaty. Stewart Raby has written two useful articles, "Indian Land Surrenders in Southern Saskatchewan" [193] and "Indian Treaty No. Five and the Pas Agency, Saskatchewan, N.W.T." [192]. The Indian perspective on the treaties is found in Richard Price, ed., *The Spirit of the Alberta Indian Treaties* [191]. René Fumoleau, O.M.I., provides a longer account in *As Long as This Land Shall Last: A History of Treaty Eight and Treaty Eleven, 1870– 1939* [90]. These two particular treaties were concluded somewhat later, in 1899 and 1921.

The reserve system was also applied in western Canada, and a number of studies have examined various aspects of its application. For a brief account of the early beginnings, see John L. Taylor, "Canada's North-West Indian Policy in the 1870's: Traditional Promises and Necessary Innovations" [251]. John L. Tobias's "Indian Reserves in Western Canada: Indian Homelands or Devices for Assimilation" [253] also traces the origin and early application of the western reserve system. The roles of two early Indian agents are examined in A. J. Looy, "Saskatchewan's First Indian Agent, M. G. Dickieson" [163], and in Jean Larmour, "Edgar Dewdney: Indian Commissioner in the Transition Period of Indian Settlement 1879– 1884" [155]. Other aspects of policy are examined in Jacqueline Gresko, "White 'Rites' and Indian 'Rites': Indian Education and Native Responses in the West, 1870– 1910" [104] and in D. M. McLeod, "Liquor Control in the North-West Territories: The Permit System, 1870– 91" [171].

Considerable attention has been given to Indian– government– White relations in the years that led up to the 1885 armed conflict. Paul F. Sharp, "Massacre at Cypress Hills" [224], and P. Goldring, "The Cypress Hills Massacre: A Century's Retrospect" [95], both examine that dramatic, and tragic, episode. Sharp's *Whoop-up Country* [225] is also good concerning the massacre. Isabel Andrews examined another aspect of the period in "Indian Protest against Starvation: The Yellow Calf Incident of 1884" [6]. Further background reading should include Norma Sluman's *Blackfoot Crossing* [227] and her imaginative biography *Poundmaker* [228], as well as Robert Jefferson, *Fifty Years on the Saskatchewan* [142].

Sluman's *Poundmaker* [228], William B. Fraser's "Big Bear, Indian Patriot" [88], and Robert S. Allen's "Big Bear" [3] have good accounts of the rebellion itself. Stuart Hughes has edited *The Frog Lake "Massacre": Personal Perspectives on Ethnic Conflict* [130]. Jean Larmour, "Edgar Dewdney and the Aftermath of the Rebellion" [154], and Sandra E. Bingaman, "The Trials of Poundmaker and Big Bear, 1885" [13], provide two further accounts of the Indian protest. Desmond Morton, *The Last War Drum* [179], is certainly among the best military accounts of the rebellion as a whole.

Studies that deal specifically with Indian affairs in

western Canada in the postrebellion era are fairly rare. Attention should be drawn, however, to David Hall, "Clifford Sifton and Canadian Indian Administration, 1896–1905" [107]. *One Century Later: Western Canadian Reserve Indians Since Treaty Seven*, edited by Ian A. L. Getty and Donald B. Smith [92], contains chapters by Arthur J. Ray [196], Hugh A. Dempsey [70], Stan Cuthand [65], and George F. G. Stanley [244] concerning various aspects of Indian affairs in western Canada over the past century.

British Columbia

British Columbia entered Confederation in 1871, at which point responsibility for Indian affairs in the province passed to the federal government. Regrettably, no established and constant policy regarding Indians or Indian lands had been set in the colonial period. Some effort regarding land had been made by James Douglas. As chief factor of the Hudson's Bay Company, he negotiated and concluded some fourteen treaties with the Indians of Vancouver Island for the surrender of land. Later, as governor of the colony of Vancouver Island and mainland British Columbia, he enunciated the desirability of reserving tracts for exclusive Indian use, and he instructed his surveyor to lay out large areas as Indian reserves. But he did not, as governor, secure any land surrenders: nor did he specify a formula or policy regarding the size or location of reserves. His successors as governor had little sympathy for Indian rights and took no action whatever. Indeed, leading officials and colonists dismissed the view that Indians of British Columbia possessed land rights. Thus, although the Confederation agreement called upon the federal government to pursue "a policy as liberal as that hitherto pursued by the British Columbia Government," the reality was that the policy had been quite illiberal regarding land.

The story of the colonial period is set forth briefly in Surtees, *The Original People* [246], and somewhat more fully in Wilson Duff, *The Indian History of British Columbia* [74], and Cumming and Mickenberg, *Native Rights in Canada*, 2d ed. [64]. In the years after 1871 the land question grew more complicated. The federal government attempted to establish and apply policy, but it met with resistance from provincial authorities, who held firm to the view that Indians possessed no proprietary claim to land. A number of fine studies have dealt with this issue.

Perhaps the most vocal, and effective, opponent of Indian rights to land was Joseph W. Trutch, who was land commissioner in the colonial period, a leader of the Confederation movement, and later the lieutenant governor of the province. His role is discussed in a paper by Robin Fisher, "Joseph Trutch and Indian Land Policy" [84]. Fisher followed this with "An Exercise in Futility: The Joint Committee on Indian Land in British Columbia, 1875–1880" [85], which deals with an early effort to settle the land issue. His more recent *Contact and Conflict: Indian-European Relations in British*

Columbia, 1774–1890 [86] treats the wider subject of Indian-White relations, and does it well. Wilson Duff's *The Indian History of British Columbia*, volume 1, *The Impact of the White Man* [74], also embraces the wider topic. Although somewhat abrupt in its treatment, Duff's book deals with both the colonial period and the national period and provides the best entry into the topic for the uninitiated. His examination, "The Fort Victoria Treaties" [73], is a more complete study of the Douglas treaties.

The Struggle for Survival: Indian Cultures and the Protestant Ethic in British Columbia, by Forrest E. La Violette [157] is an excellent account of Indian affairs and Indian policy in British Columbia. First issued in 1961 and reprinted in 1973, it treats the land question at considerable length; and it examines policy in general, with specific attention accorded to government—and missionary—efforts to supress the potlatch, unique to the Pacific coast. Robert E. Cail, *Land, Man and Law: The Disposal of Crown Lands in British Columbia, 1871–1913* [20], devotes three chapters to imperial Indian policy and post-Confederation land policy, and Patterson, *The Canadian Indian* [183], accords a full chapter to British Columbia. Other studies that treat specific aspects of policy and Indian affairs in British Columbia include the following: W. Garland Foster, "British Columbia Indian Lands" [87]; Kenneth Lysyk, "Indian Hunting Rights: Constitutional Considerations and the Role of Indian Treaties in British Columbia" [165]; E. Palmer Patterson II, "Andrew Paull (1890–1959):

Finding a Voice for the New Indian" [184], and his "Andrew Paull and the Early History of British Columbia Indian Organizations" [185]; Jean Usher, *William Duncan of Metlakatla: A Victorian Missionary in British Columbia* [276]; and, Rolf Knight, *Indians at Work: An Informal History of Native Indian Labour in British Columbia, 1858–1930* [152].

The White Paper

The most dramatic proposals concerning Indian policy since 1830 came in 1969 when the Honorable Jean Chrétien, then minister of Indian affairs, offered the *Statement of the Government of Canada on Indian Policy* [32] in the House of Commons. This statement, popularly referred to as the White Paper, resulted from a variety of causes, including criticisms of the paternal nature of Indian administration. Criticisms and questions concerning policy had been expressed in such studies as the two-volume *Survey of Contemporary Indians of Canada*, edited by Harry B. Hawthorn [112]; *The Economic Impact of the Public Sector upon the Indians of British Columbia*, prepared by D. B. Fields and W. T. Stanbury [80]; Ella Cork, *The Worst of the Bargain* [56]; D. M. Hurley, *Report on Indian Land Rights in the Atlantic Provinces* [132]: G. Challies, *The Law of Expropriation* [48]; Heather Robertson, *Reservations Are for Indians* [199]; H. E. Staats, "Some Aspects of the Legal Status of Canadian Indians" [233]; and, Malcolm Montgomery, "The Legal Status of the Six Nations in Canada" [175].

The White Paper called for the repeal of the Indian Act, the abolition of the Indian Department, the transfer of responsibility for Indian affairs to the provincial governments, and the transfer of control of Indian lands to the Indian people themselves. This proposed policy not only evoked an angry response from many Indian leaders and organizations, but also sparked a renewed interest generally in the subject of Indian policy and Indian affairs.

Indian response was most articulately expressed by Harold Cardinal's *The Unjust Society* [46], which rejected the White Paper and concurrently outlined weaknesses in the old policy; by *Citizens Plus* [134], which the Indian chiefs of Alberta presented to the prime minister in 1970; and by Waubageshig's (Harvey McCue) collection of readings, *The Only Good Indian* [282]. A minority Indian view was expressed in William I. C. Wuttunee, *Ruffled Feathers* [289]. *Beyond Traplines*, by Charles E. Hendry [119], sponsored by the Anglican church of Canada, also questioned the new policy. A subsequent Anglican church publication, *Bulletin 201* [7], reproduced statements by Indians and some replies by government officials, including Jean Chrétien.

Because of the vocal, and almost unanimous, opposition, the White Paper was not implemented. Nor is it likely to be. In the decade since its introduction, however, considerable research and study has been directed toward Indian affairs and Indian policy, both past and current, in Canada. Much of it regrettably, is still in thesis form, and one hopes that this work will soon find its way into print. Also to be anticipated are two studies in progress. One is *History of the Indians of Ontario* [202], being prepared under the general editorship of Edward S. Rogers of the Ethnohistory section of the Royal Ontario Museum. It will form one of the publications of the Ontario Historical Studies Series. The *Atlas of Great Lakes Indian History* [250], a current project of the Newberry Library under the direction of Dr. Helen H. Tanner, will provide an excellent geographic and cartographic background for the Canadian policy in the region of the Great Lakes. Recently completed is a fine study by Sally Weaver entitled *Making Canadian Indian Policy: The Hidden Agenda, 1968–1970* [283], an analytical examination of the formulation of the White Paper of 1969 and its aftermath. Another recent study that bears mentioning is *Our Land: The Maritimes* [98], edited by G. P. Gould and R. G. Semple, which outlines the basis of Indian claims in the Maritime provinces. Less recent, but important because it treats Indian affairs in terms of federal-provincial jurisdictions, is Jacques Rousseau's "The Northern Quebec Eskimo Problem and the Ottawa-Quebec Struggle" [210].

Harold Cardinal's second book, *The Rebirth of Canada's Indians* [47], concerns itself with revisions of the Indian Act and a critique of education policy and Indian organizations. James Burke's *Paper Tomahawks: From Red Tape to Red Power* [17] is a good critique of federal government policy and of Indian leaders. The plight of Indian women is outlined in Kathleen Jamieson, *Indian Women and the Law in Canada: Citizens*

Minus [141], and in *Speaking Together: Canada's Native Women*, edited by Jean Goodwill [97]. Of particular concern, of course, are the Indian Act regulations that force automatic enfranchisement on Indian women who marry non-Indians. Emma La Roque, *Defeathering the Indian* [156], is a commentary, based on personal experience, on education received by Indians and about Indians, in which she pleads for an end to the stereotyping of Indians. Douglas Sanders, who supervised the preparation of the first edition of *Native Rights in Canada*, has published two important articles regarding the legal aspects of Indian land rights and Indian status: "The Bill of Rights and Indian Status" [214] and "The Nishga Case" [215]. Regarding education, in 1972 the National Indian Brotherhood presented its document *Indian Control of Indian Education* [180] to the minister of Indian affairs. A very recent study is J. Rick Ponting and Roger Gibbins, *Out of Irrelevance: A Socio-political Introduction to Indian Affairs in Canada* [188], which directs attention to activities on all fronts during the 1970s. Ponting and Gibbons have also broached a unique problem in their article, "English Canadian and French Quebeckers' Reactions to Contemporary Indian Protest" [189].

The Department of Indian Affairs itself regularly publishes reports, booklets, and statements treating contemporary or historical topics. Several of those published through the Research Branch have already been mentioned. Another that warrants special attention is that issued by the Reserves and Trusts Branch,

Atlas of Indian Reserves and Settlements, Canada 1971 [33], an ambitious undertaking that locates, names, and gives the size of every reserve in the country as of 1971. The *Atlas* was reprinted in 1978. Two studies on a specific topics by William Henderson also warrant attention. They are *Land Tenure in Indian Reserves* [116] and *Canada's Indian Reserves: The Usufruct in Our Constitution* [118]. Both were prepared for the Research Branch of the Department of Indian Affairs.

In the 1960s the department issued a series of information booklets. Of special interest was a group of five that provided a combination of ethnohistory, history, treatment, and policy concerning the Indians of each of five geographic regions of Canada: *Indians of British Columbia* [27]; *Indians of Quebec and the Maritime Provinces* [25]; *Indians of Ontario* [28]: *Indians of the Prairie Provinces* [29]; and *Indians of the Yukon and the Northern Territories* [23]. Three other booklets issued in the 1960s are still very useful, though somewhat dated. These are *Discussion Notes on the Indian Act* [31]; *Indian Affairs: Facts and Figures* [26]; and *Linguistic and Cultural Affiliations of Canadian Indian Bands* [30]. Other government publications that bear noting are the following: *Native Peoples and Justice* [43]; *The Indians and the Law* [45]; *Native Claims: Policy, Processes and Perspectives* [37]; *The Canadian Indian: A Brief Outline* [24]; *Indian Education in Canada* [35]; *Registered Indian Population by Sex and Residence* (1978) [44]; and, most recently, *Indian Conditions: A Survey* [38].

These departmental booklets reveal the aims and

policy of the present government. The outlook presented is somewhat sanguine, and they should be approached with that in mind and in conjunction with the more complete, and usually more critical, works mentioned above. It should be said, however, that the department's publications are really quite objective. They should be read with caution, but not with mistrust.

Indian policy has also become a subject of considerable interest in the elementary and secondary schools of Canada. Several textbooks have been written to meet that demand. Most of them adopt the problems approach, using readings, documents, and opinions to inspire discussion and further reading. Surtees, *The Original People* [246], has already been mentioned. Other such texts are the following: Jean L. Elliott, ed., *Minority Canadians*, volume 1, *Native Peoples* [78]; Gerald Walsh, *Indians in Transition: An Inquiry Approach* [281]; R. P. Bowes et al., *The Indian: Assimilation, Integration or Separation?* [15]; and J. S. Frideres, *Canada's Indians: Contemporary Conflicts* [89].

ALPHABETICAL LIST AND INDEX

*Denotes items suitable for secondary school students

Item No.		Essay Page No.

[1]   Abbott, Frederick H. 1915. *The Administration of Indian Affairs in Canada*. Washington, D.C.: Government Printing Office.   (45)

[2]   Alden, John R. 1940. "The Albany Congress and the Creation of the Indian Superintendencies." *Mississippi Valley Historical Review* 17:193–210.   (23)

[3]   Allen, Robert S. 1972. "Big Bear." *Saskatchewan History* 25:1–17.   (50)

*[4]   ———. 1975. *The British Indian Department and the Frontier in North America: 1755–1830*. Ottawa: Parks Canada, National Historic Parks and Sites Branch, Indian and Northern Affairs. (23, 24)

[5]   Alvord, Clarence. 1908. "The Genesis of the Proclamation of 1763." *Michigan Pioneer and Historical Society* 36:20–25.   (22)

[6]   Andrews, Isabel. 1975. "Indian Protest
        against Starvation: The Yellow Calf In-
        cident of 1884." *Saskatchewan History*
        28:41–51.   (50)

*[7]   Anglican Church of Canada. 1970.
        *Bulletin 201: Recent Statements by the In-
        dians of Canada, General Synod Action
        1969, Some Government Responses,
        Suggested Resource*. Toronto: Anglican
        Church of Canada.   (55)

[8]   Bailey, Alfred Goldsworthy. 1937. *The
        Conflict of European and Eastern Algon-
        kian Cultures, 1504–1700: A Study in
        Canadian Civilization*. Sackville: Tribune
        Press. 2d ed., Toronto: University of
        Toronto Press, 1969.   (3)

[9]   Bannon, Rev. Richard V. 1952. "An-
        toine Gaulin, 1674–1770: An Apostle
        of Early Acadie." *Canadian Catholic His-
        torical Association Report* 19:49–59.   (20)

[10]   Bartlett, Richard H. 1978. "The Indian
        Act of Canada." *Buffalo Law Review*
        27:581–616.   (45)

[11]   Beatty, W. W. 1946. "The Goal of In-
        dian Assimilation." *Canadian Journal of
        Economics and Political Science* 12:395–
        404.   (47)

[12]   Belliveau, Pierre. 1962. "Indians and Some Raids on Massachusetts about 1690–1704." *Société Historique Acadienne*, deuxième cahier, 1:15–33.   (20)

[13]   Bingaman, Sandra Estlin. 1975. "The Trials of Poundmaker and Big Bear, 1885." *Saskatchewan History* 28:81–94.   (50)

[14]   Bleasdale, Ruth. 1974. "Manitowaning: An Experiment in Indian Settlement." *Ontario History* 66:147–57.   (36)

*[15]   Bowes, R. P., et al. 1972. *The Indian: Assimilation, Integration or Separation?* Scarborough, Ont.: Prentice-Hall.   (59)

[16]   Brebner, J. B., ed. 1925. "Subsidized Intermarriage with the Indians: An Incident in British Colonial Policy." *Canadian Historical Review* 6:33–36.   (39)

[17]   Burke, James. 1976. *Paper Tomahawks: From Red Tape to Red Power*. Winnipeg: Queenston House.   (56)

[18]   Burt, A. L. 1931. "A New Approach to the Problem of the Western Posts." *Canadian Historical Association Report*, pp. 61–75.   (27)

[19]   ———. 1940. *The United States, Great Britain and British North America from the Revolution to the Establishment of Peace after the War of 1812*. New Haven: Yale University Press. Reprinted, Toronto: Ryerson, 1969.   (28)

[20]   Cail, Robert E. 1974. *Land, Man and Law: The Disposal of Crown Lands in British Columbia, 1871–1913*. Vancouver: University of British Columbia Press.   (53)

[21]   Campeau, Lucien, ed. 1967. *La première mission d'Acadie*. Quebec: Presses de l'Université Laval.   (20)

[22]   Canada. 1891. *Indian Treaties and Surrenders from 1680 to 1890*. 2 vols. Ottawa: Queen's Printer. Reprinted, Toronto: S. E. Dawson, 1905; Toronto: Coles, 1973, 3 vols.   (25)

*[23]   Canada. Department of Indian Affairs and Northern Development. 1965. *Indians of the Yukon and the Northern Territories*. Ottawa: Queen's Printer. Revised and reprinted as *The Canadian Indian: Yukon and the Northwest Territories*. Ottawa: Indian and Northern Affairs, 1973.   (58)

*[24]   ———. 1966. *The Canadian Indian: A Brief Outline*. Ottawa: Indian and Northern Affairs, 1975.   (58)

*[25]   ———. 1966. *Indians of Quebec and the Maritime Provinces*. Ottawa: Queen's Printer. Revised and reprinted as *The Canadian Indian: Quebec and the Atlantic Provinces*. Ottawa: Indian and Northern Affairs, 1973.   (58)

*[26]   ———. 1967. *Indian Affairs: Facts and Figures*. Ottawa: Queen's Printer.   (58)

*[27]   ———. 1967. *Indians of British Columbia*. Ottawa: Queen's Printer.   (58)

*[28]   ———. 1967. *Indians of Ontario*. Ottawa: Queen's Printer.   (58)

*[29]   ———. 1967. *Indians of the Prairie Provinces*. Ottawa: Queen's Printer.   (58)

*[30]   ———. 1967. *Linguistic and Cultural Affiliations of Canadian Indian Bands*. Ottawa: Queen's Printer.   (58)

*[31]   ———. 1968. *Discussion Notes on the Indian Act*. Ottawa: Queen's Printer.   (58)

*[32]   ——. 1969. *Statement of the Government of Canada on Indian Policy*. Ottawa: Queen's Printer.   (54)

*[33]   ——. 1971. *Atlas of Indian Reserves and Settlements, Canada 1971*. Ottawa: Indian and Northern Affairs. Reprinted 1978.   (58)

*[34]   ——. 1973. *History of Indian Policy*. Background Paper no. 2. Ottawa: Indian and Northern Affairs.   (45)

*[35]   ——. 1973. *Indian Education in Canada*. Ottawa: Indian and Northern Affairs.   (58)

*[36]   ——. 1973. *Indian Status: What Is the Present Law?* Background Paper no. 1. Ottawa: Indian and Northern Affairs.   (45)

*[37]   ——. 1978. *Native Claims: Policy, Processes and Perspectives*. Ottawa: Indian and Northern Affairs.   (58)

*[38]   ——. 1980. *Indian Conditions: A Survey*. Ottawa: Indian and Northern Affairs.   (58)

[39]   Canada. Geographic Board. 1913.

Handbook of Indians of Canada: Appendix to the Tenth Report of the Geographic Board of Canada. Ottawa: King's Printer. Reprinted, Toronto: Coles, 1971. Published in French as *Manuel des Indiens du Canada publié comme appendix au dixième rapport du Bureau Géographique du Canada.* Ottawa: King's Printer, 1915. (3)

[40] Canada. Legislative Assembly. 1844–45. *Report on the Affairs of the Indians in Canada.* Sections 1 and 2. Journals, Legislative Assembly, Canada, Appendix EEE. (35, 37)

[41] ———. 1847. *Report on the Affairs of the Indians in Canada.* Section 3. Journals, Legislative Assembly, Canada, Appendix T. (35, 37)

[42] ———. 1858. *Report of the Special Commissioners to Investigate Indian Affairs in Canada.* Sessional Papers, Appendix 21. (35, 37)

[43] Canada. Ministry of the Solicitor General. 1975. *Native Peoples and Justice.* Ottawa: Communications Division, Ministry of the Solicitor General. (58)

[44] Canada. Statistics Division. 1978. *Regis-*

tered Indian Population by Sex and Residence. Ottawa: Programme Reference Center, IIAP. This publication is updated annually, (58)

*[45] Canadian Corrections Association. 1967. *The Indians and the Law*. Ottawa: Queen's Printer. (58)

*[46] Cardinal, Harold. 1969. *The Unjust Society*. Edmonton: Hurtig. (46, 55)

[47] ———. 1977. *The Rebirth of Canada's Indians*. Edmonton: Hurtig. (56)

[48] Challies, G. 1963. *The Law of Expropriation*. Montreal: Wilson and LaFleur. (54)

[49] Chinard, Gilbert. 1913. *L'Amérique et le rêve exotique dans la littérature française au dix-septième et au dix-huitième siècle*. Paris: Hachette. Reprinted, Geneva: Slatkine Reprints, 1970. (6)

[50] Clark, Andrew Hill. 1968. *Acadia: The Geography of Early Nova Scotia to 1760*. Madison: University of Wisconsin Press. (19)

[51] Clifton, James A. 1975. *A Place of Ref-*

uge for All Time: Migration of the American Potawatomi into Upper Canada, 1830 to 1850. National Museum of Man Mercury Series, Canadian Ethnology Service Paper no. 26. Ottawa: National Museums of Canada.   (32)

[52]   ———. 1978. "Merchant, Soldier, Broker, Chief: A Corrected Obituary of Captain Billy Caldwell." *Journal of the Illinois State Historical Society* 71:185–210.   (29)

*[53]   ———. 1979. "'Visiting Indians' in Canada." Manuscript on file in Canadian Ethnology Service, National Museum of Man, Ottawa.   (27)

[54]   Coleman, Emma Lewis. 1925. *New England Captives Carried to Canada between 1677 and 1760 during the French and Indian Wars.* 2 vols. Portland: Southworth Press.   (15)

[55]   Conkling, Robert. 1974. "Legitimacy and Conversion in Social Change: The Case of the French Missionaries and the Northeastern Algonkian." *Ethnohistory* 21:1–24.   (20)

[56]   Cork, Ella. 1962. *The Worst of the Bar-gain*. San Jacinto, Calif.: Foundation for Social Research.   (54)

*[57]   Craig, Gerald M. 1963. *Upper Canada: The Formative Years, 1784–1841*. Toronto: McClelland and Steward.   (25)

[58]   Cruickshank, E. A. 1895. "The Employment of Indians in the War of 1812." *American Historical Association Report,* pp. 321–35.   (30)

[59]   ———. 1927. "The 'Chesapeake' Crisis as It Affected Upper Canada." *Ontario Historical Society Papers and Records* 24:281–322.   (30)

*[60]   ———. 1930. "The Coming of the Loyalist Mohawks to the Bay of Quinté." *Ontario Historical Society Papers and Records* 26:390–403.   (26)

[61]   ———, ed. 1902. "Campaigns of 1812–14: Contemporary Narratives by Captain W. H. Merritt, Colonel William Claus, Lieut.-Colonel Matthew Elliott, and Captain John Norton." *Niagara Historical Society Publications* 9:5–22.   (31)

[62]   ——, ed. 1923–30. *Correspondence of Lieutenant-Governor John Graves Simcoe*. 5 vols. Toronto: Ontario Historical Society.   (26)

[63]   Cruickshank, E. A., and A. F. Hunter, eds. 1932–36. *Correspondence of the Honourable Peter Russell*. 3 vols. Toronto: Ontario Historical Society.   (26)

[64]   Cumming, Peter A., and Neil H. Mickenberg, eds. 1972. *Native Rights in Canada*. 2d ed. Toronto: General Publishing Company.   (2, 22, 45, 52)

[65]   Cuthand, Stan. 1978. "The Native Peoples of the Prairie Provinces in the 1920's and the 1930's." In *One Century Later: Western Canadian Reserve Indians since Treaty Seven*, ed. Ian A. L. Getty and Donald B. Smith, pp. 31–42. Vancouver: University of British Columbia Press.   (51)

[66]   Daugherty, Wayne. 1980. *Maritime Indian Treaties in Historical Perspective*. Ottawa: Research Branch, Department of Indian and Northern Affairs.   (41)

[67]   Daugherty, Wayne, and Dennis Madill.

1980. *Indian Government under Indian Act Legislation, 1868–1951*. Ottawa: Research Branch, Department of Indian and Northern Affairs. (47)

[68] David, Albert. 1929. "Messire Pierre Maillard, apôtre des Micmacs." *Bulletin des Recherches Historiques* 35:365–75. (20)

[69] ———. 1935. "L'apôtre des Micmacs." *Revue du l'Université d'Ottawa.* 5:49–82. (20)

[70] Dempsey, Hugh A. 1978. "One Hundred Years of Treaty Seven." In *One Century Later: Western Canadian Reserve Indians since Treaty Seven*, ed. Ian A. L. Getty and Donald B. Smith, pp. 20–30. Vancouver: University of British Columbia Press. (51)

[71] Derosiers, Leo-Paul. 1947. *Iroquoisie*. Vol. 1. *1534–1646*. Montreal: Institut d'Histoire de l'Amérique Française. (9)

*[72] Dickason, Olive Patricia. 1976. *Louisbourg and the Indians: A Study in Imperial Race Relations, 1713–1760*. Ottawa: Parks Canada. (7, 12, 21)

[73] Duff, Wilson. 1969. "The Fort Victoria Treaties." *BC Studies* 3:3–57. (53)

*[74]   ———. 1969. *The Indian History of British Columbia*. Vol. 1. *The Impact of the White Man*. 2d ed. Anthropology in British Columbia, Memoir no. 5. Victoria: Provincial Museum of Natural History and Anthropology.   (52, 53)

[75]   Eccles, W. J. 1959. *Frontenac: The Courtier Governor*. Toronto: McClelland and Stewart.   (15)

[76]   ———. 1964. *Canada under Louis XIV, 1663–1701*. Toronto: McClelland and Stewart.   (15)

[77]   ———. 1969. *The Canadian Frontier, 1534–1760*. Toronto: Holt, Rinehart and Winston.   (16, 18, 19)

*[78]   Elliott, Jean Leonard, ed. 1971. *Minority Canadians*. Vol. 1. *Native Peoples*. Scarborough, Ont.: Prentice-Hall.   (59)

[79]   Erasmus, Peter. 1976. *Buffalo Days and Nights*. As told to Henry Thompson, ed. Irene Spry. Calgary: Glenbow-Alberta Institute.   (49)

[80]   Fields, D. B., and W. T. Stanbury. 1970. *The Economic Impact of the Public*

Sector upon the Indians of British Columbia: An Examination of the Incidence of Taxation and Expenditure of Three Levels of Government. Vancouver: University of British Columbia Press.   (54)

[81]   Fingard, Judith. 1972. "The New England Company and the New Brunswick Indians, 1786–1826: A Comment on the Colonial Perversion of British Benevolence." *Acadiensis* 1(2):29–42.   (40)

[82]   ———. 1973 "English Humanitarianism and the Colonial Mind: Walter Bromley in Nova Scotia, 1813–1825." *Canadian Historical Review* 54:123–51.   (40)

[83]   Firth, E. G. 1956. "The Administration of Peter Russell, 1796–1799." *Ontario History* 48:163–81.   (27)

[84]   Fisher, Robin. 1971–72. "Joseph Trutch and Indian Land Policy." *BC Studies* 12:3–33.   (52)

[85]   ———. 1975. "An Exercise in Futility: The Joint Commission on Indian Land in British Columbia, 1875–1880." *Canadian Historical Association Papers* 5:79–94.   (52)

[86]   ———. 1977. *Contact and Conflict: Indian-European Relations in British Columbia, 1774–1890*. Vancouver: University of British Columbia Press. Reprinted 1978.   (52)

[87]   Foster, W. Garland. 1937. "British Columbia Indian Lands." *Pacific Northwest Quarterly* 28:151–62.   (53)

*[88]   Fraser, William B. 1966. "Big Bear, Indian Patriot." *Alberta Historical Review* 14:1–13.   (50)

*[89]   Frideres, J. S. 1974. *Canada's Indians: Contemporary Conflicts*. Scarborough, Ont.: Prentice-Hall.   (59)

[90]   Fumoleau, René, O.M.I. 1973. *As Long as This Land Shall Last: A History of Treaty Eight and Treaty Eleven, 1870–1939*. Toronto: McClelland and Stewart.   (49)

[91]   Gates, Lillian F. 1968. *Land Policies of Upper Canada*. Toronto: University of Toronto Press.   (25)

[92]   Getty, Ian A. L., and Donald B. Smith, eds. 1978. *One Century Later: Western Canadian Reserve Indians since Treaty Sev-*

en. Vancouver: University of British Columbia Press. (51)

[93] Gilpin, Alec R. 1958. *The War of 1812 in the Old Northwest.* East Lansing: Michigan State University Press. Reprinted, Toronto: Ryerson Press, 1968. (31)

[94] Giraud, Marcel. 1945. *Le métis canadien: Son rôle dans l'historie des provinces de l'ouest.* Paris: Institut d'Ethnologie. (17)

[95] Goldring, P. 1973. "The Cypress Massacre: A Century's Retrospect." *Saskatchewan History* 26:81–102. (50)

[96] Goldstein, Robert A. 1969. *French-Iroquois Diplomatic and Military Relations, 1609–1701.* The Hague and Paris: Mouton. (9)

[97] Goodwill, Jean, ed. 1975. *Speaking Together: Canada's Native Women.* Ottawa: Secretary of State. (57)

[98] Gould, G. P., and R. G. Semple, eds. 1980. *Our Land: The Maritimes.* Fredericton, N.B.: Saint Anne's Point Press. (56)

*[99] Graham, Elizabeth. 1975. *Medicine Man*

to Missionary: Missionaries as Agents for Change among the Indians of Southern Ontario 1784–1867. Toronto: Peter Martin Associates. (36)

[100] Graham, G. S. 1934. "The Indian Menace and the Retention of the Western Posts." *Canadian Historical Review* 15:46–48. (28)

[101] Gray, Elma E., and Leslie Robb Gray. 1956. *Wilderness Christians: The Moravian Mission to the Delaware Indians*. Toronto: Macmillan. (32)

[102] Gray, Leslie Robb. 1955. "The Moravian Missionaries, Their Indians, and the Canadian Government." *Canadian Historical Association Annual Report*, pp. 96–104. (32)

[103] Graymont, Barbara. 1972. *The Iroquois in the American Revolution*. Syracuse: Syracuse University Press. (24)

[104] Gresko, Jacqueline. 1974. "White 'Rites' and Indian 'Rites': Indian Education and Native Responses in the West, 1870–1910." In *Western Canada: Past and Present*, ed. A. W. Rasporitch, pp.

163–82. Calgary: McClelland and
Stewart West.   (50)

[105]   Groulx, Lionel. 1949. "Missionnaries de
l'est en Nouvelle-France: Réductions et
séminaries indiens." *Revue d'Historie de
l'Amérique Français* 3:45–72.   (13)

*[106] Grumet, Robert S. 1979. *Native Ameri-
cans of the Northwest Coast: A Critical Bibliography.* Bloomington and London:
Indiana University Press for Newberry
Library.   (4)

[107]   Hall, David. 1972. "Clifford Sifton and
Canadian Indian Administration,
1896–1905." *Prarie Forum* 2:127–51.   (51)

[108]   Harper, Allen G. 1945. "Canada's Indian Administration: Basic Concepts
and Objectives." *America Indigena*
5:119–32.   (46)

[109]   ———. 1946. "Canada's Indian Administration: The Indian Act." *America Indigena* 6:297–314.   (46)

[110]   ———. 1947. "Canada's Indian Administration: The Treaty System." *America
Indigena* 7:129–48.   (46)

[111]   Harvey, D. C. 1926. *The French Régime in Prince Edward Island*. New Haven: Yale University Press.   (21)

[112]   Hawthorn, Harry B., ed. 1966– 67. *A Survey of Contemporary Indians of Canada: Economic, Political, Educational Needs and Policies*. 2 vols. Ottawa: Indian Affairs Branch.   (54)

[113]   Healy, George R. 1958. "The French Jesuits and the Idea of the Noble Savage." *William and Mary Quarterly*, 3d ser., 15:143– 67.   (6)

*[114]   Heidenreich, Conrad. 1971. *Huronia: A History and Geography of the Huron Indians, 1600– 1650*. Toronto: McClelland and Stewart.   (10)

[115]   Helm, June. 1976. *The Indians of the Subarctic: A Critical Bibliography*. Bloomington and London: Indiana University Press for Newberry Library.   (3)

[116]   Henderson, William B. 1978. *Land Tenure in Indian Reserves*. Ottawa: Research Branch, Indian and Northern Affairs.   (58)

[117]   ———. 1980. *Canada's Indian Reserves:*

Pre-Confederation. Ottawa: Research Branch, Indian and Northern Affairs. (37, 38)

[118] ———. 1980. *Canada's Indian Reserves: The Usufruct in Our Constitution*. Ottawa: Research Branch, Indian and Northern Affairs. (58)

*[119] Hendry, Charles E. 1969. *Beyond Traplines*. Toronto: Anglican Church of Canada. (55)

[120] Herrington, M. Eleanor. 1921. "Captain John Deserontyou and the Mohawk Settlement at Deseronto." *Queen's Quarterly* 29:165–80. (26)

[121] Hodgetts, J. E. 1965. *Pioneer Public Service: An Administrative History of the United Canadas, 1841–1867*. Toronto: University of Toronto Press. (35)

[122] Hoebel, E. Adamson. 1977. *The Plains Indians: A Critical Bibliography*. Bloomington and London: Indiana University Press for Newberry Library. (4)

[123] Horsman, Reginald. 1958. "British Indian Policy in the Northwest, 1807–1812." *Mississippi Valley Historical Review* 45:51–66. (30)

[124]   ———. 1961. "The British Indian Department and the Abortive Treaty of Lower Sandusky, 1793." *Ohio Historical Quarterly* 70:189–213.   (28)

[125]   ———. 1962. "The British Indian Department and the Resistance to General Anthony Wayne, 1793–1795." *Mississippi Valley Historical Review* 49:269–91.   (28)

[126]   ———. 1964. *Matthew Elliott: British Indian Agent.* Detroit: Wayne State University Press.   (28)

[127]   ———. 1967. *Expansion and American Indian Policy, 1783–1812.* East Lansing: Michigan State University Press.   (30)

[128]   ———. 1970. *The Frontier in the Formative Years, 1783–1815.* New York: Holt, Rinehart and Winston.   (28)

[129]   Howley, James P. 1915. *The Beothuks or Red Indians: The Aboriginal Inhabitants of Newfoundland.* Cambridge: Cambridge University Press.   (41)

[130]   Hughes, Stuart. 1976. *The Frog Lake "Massacre": Personal Perspectives on*

Ethnic Conflict. Toronto: McClelland and Stewart. (50)

[131] Hunt, George T. 1940. *The Wars of the Iroquois: A Study in Intertribal Trade Relations.* Madison: University of Wisconsin Press. Reprinted 1960. (9, 15)

[132] Hurley, D. M. 1962. *Report on Indian Land Rights in the Atlantic Provinces.* Ottawa: National Museum of Man. (54)

[133] Hutton, Elizabeth Ann. 1963. "Indian Affairs in Nova Scotia, 1760–1843." *Collections of the Nova Scotia Historical Society* 34:33–54. (39)

*[134] Indian Chiefs of Alberta. 1970. *Citizens Plus.* Edmonton: Indian Association of Alberta. (55)

[135] Jacobs, Wilbur R. 1950. *Diplomacy and Indian Gifts: Anglo-French Rivalry along the Ohio and Northwestern Frontier, 1748–1763.* Stanford: Stanford University Press. Reprinted as *Wilderness Politics and Indian Gifts: The Northern Colonial Frontier, 1748–1763.* Lincoln: University of Nebraska Press, 1966. (18, 23, 27)

[136]   Jaenen, Cornelius J. 1966. "Problems of Assimilation in New France, 1603–1645." *French Historical Studies* 4:265–89.   (12)

[137]   ———. 1969. "The Frenchification and Evangelization of the Amerindians in Seventeenth Century New France." *Canadian Catholic Historical Association Study Sessions* 35:57–71.   (11)

[138]   ———. 1973. "The Meeting of the French and Amerindians in the Seventeenth Century." *Revue de l'Université d'Ottawa* 43:128–44.   (6, 12)

[139]   ———. 1974. "Amerindian Views of French Culture in the Seventeenth Century." *Canadian Historical Review* 55:261–81.   (12)

[140]   ———. 1976. *Friend and Foe: Aspects of French-Amerindian Cultural Contact in the Sixteenth and Seventeenth Centuries.* Toronto: McClelland and Stewart.   (5)

*[141]   Jamieson, Kathleen. 1978. *Indian Women and the Law in Canada: Citizens Minus.* Ottawa: Minister of Supply and Services Canada.   (57)

*[142] Jefferson, Robert. 1929. *Fifty Years on the Saskatchewan*. Battleford: Canadian North-West Historical Society.   (50)

*[143] Jenness, Diamond. 1932. *The Indians of Canada*. Ottawa: King's Printer. Reprinted, 7th ed., Ottawa: Queen's Printer, 1967.   (3)

[144] Johnson, Micheline Dumont. 1970. *Apôtres ou agitateurs: La France missionnaire en Acadie*. Trois-Rivières: Boréal Express.   (20)

[145] ———. 1974. "Pierre Maillard." In *Dictionary of Canadian Biography*, 3:415–19. Toronto: University of Toronto Press.   (20)

[146] Johnston, Charles M. 1963. "Joseph Brant, the Grand River Lands, and the Northwest Crisis." *Ontario History* 55:267–82.   (27)

[147] ———. 1964. *The Valley of the Six Nations: A Collection of Documents on the Indian Lands of the Grand River*. Toronto: Champlain Society.   (26, 33)

[148] ———. 1965. "William Claus and John Norton: A Struggle for Power in Old Ontario." *Ontario History* 57:101–8.   (27)

[149]   Jones, Peter [Kahkewaquonaby]. 1860.
         *Life and Journals of Kah-Ke-Wa-Quo-Na-
         By (Rev. Peter Jones)*. Toronto: Wesleyan
         Printing Establishment.   (32)

[150]   Kennedy, J. H. 1950. *Jesuit and Savage
         in New France*. New Haven: Yale Uni-
         versity Press.   (6)

[151]   Klinck, Carl F., and James J. Talman,
         eds. 1970. *The Journal of Major John
         Norton, 1816*. Toronto: Champlain
         Society.   (31)

[152]   Knight, Rolf. 1978. *Indians at Work: An
         Informal History of Native Indian Labour
         in British Columbia, 1858–1930*. Van-
         couver: New Star Books.   (54)

[153]   Landon, Fred, ed. 1930. "Selections
         from the Papers of James Evans, Mis-
         sionary to the Indians." *Ontario Histori-
         cal Society Papers and Records* 26:47–70. (32)

[154]   Larmour, Jean. 1970. "Edgar Dewdney
         and the Aftermath of the Rebellion."
         Saskatchewan History 23:105–17.   (50)

[155]   ———. 1980. "Edgar Dewdney: Indian
         Commissioner in the Transition Period

of Indian Settlement, 1879–1884." *Saskatchewan History* 33:13–24. (49)

*[156]   La Roque, Emma. 1975. *Defeathering the Indian.* Agincourt, Ont.: Book Society of Canada. (57)

[157]   La Violette, Forrest E. 1961. *The Struggle for Survival: Indian Cultures and the Protestant Ethic in British Columbia.* Toronto: University of Toronto Press. Reprinted 1973. (53)

[158]   Leavitt, Orpha. 1915. "British Policy on the Canadian Frontier, 1782–92: Mediation and an Indian Buffer State." *Proceedings of the Wisconsin Historical Society,* pp. 151–85. (29)

[159]   LeBlanc, Peter G. 1968. "Indian-Missionary Contact in Huronia, 1615–1649." *Ontario History* 60:133–46. (9)

[160]   Leighton, Douglas. 1977. "The Manitoulin Incident of 1863: An Indian-White Confrontation in the Province of Canada." *Ontario History* 69:113–24. (36)

*[161]   Leslie, John, and Ron Maguire, eds. 1978. *The Historical Development of the*

Indian Act. 2d ed. Ottawa: Research
Branch, Indian and Northern Affairs. (38, 45)

[162] Lewis, Rundall M. 1956. "The Manitoulin Letters of Rev. Charles Crosbie
Brough." *Ontario History* 48:63–80.   (35)

[163] Looy, A. J. 1979. "Saskatchewan's First
Indian Agent, M. G. Dickieson." *Saskatchewan History* 32:105–15.   (49)

[164] Loram, C. T., and T. F. McIlwraith,
eds. 1943. *The North American Indian Today.* University of Toronto–Yale University Seminar Conference, Toronto,
4–16 September 1939. Toronto: University of Toronto Press.   (47)

[165] Lysyk, Kenneth. 1966. "Indian Hunting Rights: Constitutional Considerations and the Role of Indian
Treaties in British Columbia." *University
of British Columbia Law Review* 2:401–
21.   (53)

[166] McDougall, John. 1970. *Opening the
Great West: Experiences of a Missionary in
1875–76.* Calgary: Glenbow-Alberta
Institute.   (49)

[167]   MacFarlane, R. O. 1934. "Indian Trade
        in Nova Scotia to 1764." *Canadian His-*
        torical Association Report, pp. 57–67.   (39)

[168]   ———. 1938. "British Indian Policy in
        Nova Scotia to 1760." *Canadian Histori-*
        cal Review 19:154–67.   (39)

[169]   McGee, H. F., ed. 1974. *The Native*
        Peoples of Atlantic Canada: A History of
        Ethnic Interaction. Toronto: McClelland
        and Stewart.   (41)

[170]   MacInnes, T. R. L. 1946. "History of
        Indian Administration in Canada."
        Canadian Journal of Economics and Politi-
        cal Science 12:387–94.   (47)

[171]   McLeod, D. M. 1963. "Liquor Control
        in the North-West Territories: The
        Permit System, 1870–91." *Saskatchewan*
        History 16:81–89.   (50)

[172]   Mahon, John K. 1972. *The War of 1812.*
        Gainsville: University of Florida Press.   (31)

[173]   Maillard, Pierre Antoine Simon. 1863.
        "Lettre de M. l'Abbé Maillard sur les
        missions de l'Acadie et particulièrement
        sur les missions Micmaques." In *Les*

soirées canadiennes: Recueil de littérature nationale, ed. H. Casgarain, 3:289–426.   (21)

[174]   Mellor, G. R. 1951. *British Imperial Trusteeship.* London: Faber and Faber.   (33)

[175]   Montgomery, Malcolm. 1963. "The Legal Status of the Six Nations in Canada." *Ontario History* 55:93–105.   (54)

*[176]   Morris, Alexander. 1880. *The Treaties of Canada with the Indians of Manitoba and the North-West Territories, Including the Negotiations on Which They Were Based, and Other Information Relating Thereto.* Toronto: Willing and Williamson. Reprinted, Toronto: Coles, 1971.   (48)

*[177]   Morris, J. L. 1943. *Indians of Ontario.* Toronto: Department of Lands and Forests. Reprinted 1964.   (25)

[178]   Morton, Arthur S. 1939. *A History of the Canadian West to 1870–71.* Toronto: Nelson. Reprinted, Toronto: University of Toronto Press, 1973.   (48)

*[179]   Morton, Desmond. 1972. *The Last War Drum.* Toronto: Hakkert.   (50)

*[180] National Indian Brotherhood. 1972.
        Indian Control of Indian Education. Ot-
        tawa: National Indian Brotherhood.   (57)

[181] Nelligan, Francis J. 1959. "Catholic
        Missionary Labours on the Lake
        Superior Frontier, 1667–1751." *Ontario
        History* 51:237–50.   (13)

[182] Patterson, Gilbert C. 1921. *Land Settle-
        ment in Upper Canada, 1783–1840: Six-
        teenth Report of the Department of Archives,
        Province of Ontario.* Toronto: Clarkson
        W. James.   (1, 26)

[183] Patterson, E. Palmer II. 1972. *The
        Canadian Indian: A History since 1500.*
        Don Mills, Ont.: Collier-Macmillan. (2, 21, 53)

[184] ———. 1976. "Andrew Paull (1890–
        1959): Finding a Voice for the New
        Indian." *Western Canadian Journal of An-
        thropology* 6(2):63–82.   (46, 54)

[185] ———. 1978. "Andrew Paull and the
        Early History of British Columbia In-
        dian Organizations." In *One Century La-
        ter: Western Canadian Reserve Indians
        since Treaty Seven,* ed. Ian A. L. Getty
        and Donald B. Smith, pp. 43–54. Van-

couver: University of British Columbia
Press.   (54)

[186]   Peckham, Howard H. 1947. *Pontiac and
the Indian Uprising*. Chicago: University
of Chicago Press. Reprinted 1961.   (22)

[187]   Perkins, Bradford. 1955. *The First Rapprochement: England and the United States,
1795–1805*. Philadelphia: University of
Pennsylvania Press.   (30)

[188]   Ponting, J. Rick, and Roger Gibbins.
1980. *Out of Irrelevance: A Socio-political
Introduction to Indian Affairs in Canada*.
Toronto: Butterworth.   (2, 57)

[189]   ———. 1981. "English Canadian and
French Quebeckers' Reactions to Contemporary Indian Protest." *Canadian
Review of Sociology and Anthropology*, in
press.   (57)

[190]   Price, Grenfell. 1950. *White Settlers and
Native Peoples*. Cambridge: Cambridge
University Press.   (33)

[191]   Price, Richard, ed. 1979. *The Spirit of the
Alberta Indian Treaties*. Montreal: Institute for Research on Public Policy.   (49)

[192]   Raby, Stewart. 1972. "Indian Treaty
         No. Five and the Pas Agency, Sas-
         katchewan, N.W.T." *Saskatchewan His-
         tory* 25:92–114.   (49)

[193]   ———. 1973. "Indian Land Surrenders
         in Southern Saskatchewan." *Canadian
         Geographer* 17:36–52.   (49)

*[194]   Raeman, G. E. 1967. *The Trail of the
         Iroquois Indians: How the Iroquois Nation
         Saved Canada for the British Empire*. Lon-
         don: Frederick Muller.   (24)

[195]   Ray, Arthur J. 1974. *Indians in the Fur
         Trade: Their Roles as Trappers, Hunters,
         and Middlemen in the Lands Southwest of
         Hudson Bay*. Toronto: University of To-
         ronto Press.   (48)

[196]   ———. 1978. "Fur Trade History as an
         Aspect of Native History." In *One Cen-
         tury Later: Western Canadian Reserve In-
         dians since Treaty Seven*, ed. Ian A. L.
         Getty and Donald B. Smith, pp. 7–19.
         Vancouver: University of British Co-
         lumbia Press.   (51)

[197]   Ray, Arthur J., and Donald B.
         Freeman. 1978. *"Give Us Good Measure":*

An Economic Analysis of Relations between the Indians and the Hudson's Bay Company before 1763. Toronto: University of Toronto Press.   (48)

[198]   Rich, E. E. 1958. *The History of the Hudson's Bay Company, 1670–1870.* 3 vols. London: Hudson's Bay Company Record Society.   (48)

*[199]   Robertson, Heather. 1970. *Reservations Are for Indians.* Toronto: James Larimer.   (54)

[200]   Rochemonteix, Camille de. 1895. *Les Jésuites et la Nouvelle-France au dix-septième siècle, d'après beaucoup de documents inédits.* 3 vols. Paris: Letouzey.   (13)

[201]   ———. 1906. *Les Jésuites et la Nouvelle-France au dix-huitième siècle, d'après des documents inédits.* 2 vols. Paris: A. Picard.   (13)

*[202]   Rogers, Edward S., ed. *History of the Indians of Ontario.* Ontario Historical Studies Series. Forthcoming.   (56)

[203]   Rogers, Edward S., and Flora Tobobondung. 1975. "Parry Island Farmers: A Period of Change in the Way of

Life of the Algonkians of Southern Ontario." In *Contributions to Canadian Ethnology, 1975*, ed. David B. Carlisle, pp. 247–359. National Museum of Man Mercury Series, Canadian Ethnology Service Paper no. 31. Ottawa: National Museums of Canada. (36)

[204] Rogers, Norman McL. 1930. "The Abbé Le Loutre." *Canadian Historical Review* 11:105–28. (20)

[205] Ronda, James P., and Axtell, James. 1978. *Indian Missions: A Critical Bibliography*. Bloomington and London: Indiana University Press for Newberry Library. (4)

[206] Rousseau, Jacques. 1954. "Du bon sauvage de la littérature à celui de la realité." *L'Action Universitaire* 20:12–23. (3)

[207] ———. 1958. "Ces gens qu'on dit sauvages." *Cahiers des Dix* 23:53–90. (3)

[208] ———. 1959. "Les sachems déliberent autour du feu de camp." *Cahiers des Dix* 24:9–51. (3)

[209] ———. 1960. "Les premiers canadiens." *Cahiers des Dix* 25:9–65. (3)

[210]   ———. 1969. "The Northern Quebec Eskimo Problem and the Ottawa-Quebec Struggle." *Anthropological Journal of Canada* 7:2–15.   (56)

*[211]   Rowe, Frederick W. 1977. *Extinction: The Beothuks of Newfoundland*. Toronto: McGraw-Hill Ryerson.   (41)

[212]   Rowe, S. 1905. "Anderson Record, from 1699 to 1896." *Ontario Historical Society Papers and Records* 6:109–35.   (36)

[213]   Russell, Nelson Vance. 1930. "The Indian Policy of Henry Hamilton: A Revaluation." *Canadian Historical Review* 11:20–37.   (24)

[214]   Sanders, Douglas. 1972. "The Bill of Rights and Indian Status." *University of British Columbia Law Review* 7:81–105.   (57)

[215]   ———. 1973. "The Nishga Case." *BC Studies* 19:3–20.   (57)

[216]   Schmalz, Peter S. 1977. *The History of the Saugeen Indians*. Research Publication no. 5. Ottawa: Ontario Historical Society.   (36)

[217] Scott, Abbé H.-A. 1902. *Une paroisse historique de la Nouvelle-France: Notre Dame de Sainte-Foy, 1541–1670.* Quebec: Laflamme. (14)

[218] ———. 1911. "La Bourgade Saint-Joseph de Sillery après 1670." *Nouvelle-France* 10:404–9. (14)

[219] ———. 1912. "La Bourgade Saint-Joseph de Sillery après 1670: Etablissement de Saint-Françoise-de-Sales." *Nouvelle-France* 11:224–30. (14)

*[220] Scott, Duncan D. 1914. "Indian Affairs, 1763–1841." In *Canada and Its Provinces*, ed. Adam Shortt and A. G. Doughty, 4:695–725. Toronto: Edinburgh University Press. (35)

*[221] ———. 1914. "Indian Affairs, 1840–1867." In *Canada and Its Provinces*, ed. Adam Shortt and A. G. Doughty, 5:331–62. Toronto: Edinburgh University Press. (35)

*[222] ———. 1914. "Indian Affairs, 1867–1912." In *Canada and Its Provinces*, ed. Adam Shortt and A. G. Doughty, 7:593–626. Toronto: Edinburgh University Press. (35, 45)

[223]   ———. 1931. *The Administration of Indian Affairs in Canada*. Toronto: Canadian Institute for International Affairs.   (35)

[224]   Sharp, Paul F. 1954. "Massacre at Cypress Hills." *Saskatchewan History* 7:81–99.   (50)

[225]   ———. 1955. *Whoop-up Country: The Canadian-American West, 1865–1885*. Minneapolis: University of Minnesota Press. Reprinted, Norman: University of Oklahoma Press, 1973.   (50)

[226]   Slight, Benjamin. 1844. *Indian Researches; or, Facts concerning the North American Indians: Including Notices of Their Present State of Improvement, in Their Social, Civil, and Religious Condition, with Hints for Their Future Advancement*. Montreal: Printed for the author by J. E. L. Miller.   (32)

[227]   Sluman, Norma. 1959. *Blackfoot Crossing*. Toronto: Ryerson Press.   (50)

*[228]   ———. 1967. *Poundmaker*. Toronto: Ryerson Press.   (50)

[229]   Smith, Derek G., ed. 1975. *Canadian*

Indians and the Law: Selected Documents, 1663–1972. Toronto: McClelland and Stewart.   (2)

[230] Smith, Donald B. 1974. *Le Sauvage: The Native People in Quebec: Historical Writing on the Heroic Period (1534–1663) of New France*. National Museum of Man Mercury Series, History Division Paper no. 6. Ottawa: National Museums of Canada.   (3, 6, 37)

[231] Sosin, Jack M. 1961. *Whitehall and the Wilderness: The Middle West in British Colonial Policy, 1760–1775*. Lincoln: University of Nebraska Press.   (24)

[232] ———. 1965. "The Use of Indians in the War of the American Revolution: A Re-assessment of Responsibility." *Canadian Historical Review* 46:101–21.   (24)

[233] Staats, H. E. 1964. "Some Aspects of the Legal Status of Canadian Indians." *Osgoode Hall Law Journal* 3:36–51.   (54)

[234] Stanley, George F. G. 1949. "The Policy of 'Francisation' as Applied to the Indians during the Ancien Régime." *Revue d'Histoire de l'Amérique Française* 3:333–48.   (11)

[235]   ———. 1950. "The First Indian 'Reserves' in Canada." *Revue d'Histoire de l'Amérique Française* 4:178–210.   (11, 13)

[236]   ———. 1950. "The Indians in the War of 1812." *Canadian Historical Review* 3:145–65.   (31)

[237]   ———. 1952. "The Indian Background to Canadian History." *Canadian Historical Association Report*, pp. 14–31.   (2)

[238]   ———. 1953. "The Indians and the Brandy Trade during the Ancien Régime." *Revue d'Histoire de l'Amérique Française* 6:489–505.   (11)

[239]   ———. 1960. *The Birth of Western Canada: A History of the Riel Rebellions.* Toronto: University of Toronto Press.   (48)

[240]   ———. 1960. *Canada's Soldiers.* Rev. ed. Toronto: Macmillan.   (24)

[241]   ———. 1963. "The Significance of the Six Nations' Participation in the War of 1812." *Ontario History* 55:215–31.   (31)

[242]   ———. 1964. "The Six Nations and the American Revolution." *Ontario History* 56:217–32.   (24)

[243]   ———. 1968. *New France: The Last Phase, 1744–1760*. Toronto: McClelland and Stewart.   (18)

[244]   ———. 1978. "Displaced Red Men: The Sioux in Canada." In *One Century Later: Western Canadian Reserve Indians since Treaty Seven*, ed. Ian A. L. Getty and Donald B. Smith, pp. 55–81. Vancouver: University of British Columbia Press.   (51)

[245]   Surtees, Robert J. 1969. "The Development of an Indian Reserve Policy in Canada." *Ontario History* 61:87–98.   (34)

*[246]   ———. 1971. *The Original People*. Toronto: Holt, Rinehart and Winston. (2, 52, 59)

*[247]   ———. 1977. "The Changing Image of the Canadian Indian." In *Approaches to Native History in Canada*, ed. D. A. Muise, pp. 111–25. National Museum of Man Mercury Series, History Division Paper no. 25. Ottawa: National Museums of Canada.   (17, 32)

*[248]   Symington, Fraser. 1969. *The Canadian Indian: The Illustrated History of the Great Tribes of Canada*. Toronto: McClelland and Stewart.   (viii)

[249]   Tanner, Helen Hornbeck. 1976. *The Ojibwas: A Critical Bibliography*. Bloomington and London: Indiana University Press for Newberry Library.   (3)

[250]   ———, ed. *Atlas of Great Lakes Indian History*. Norman: University of Oklahoma Press for Newberry Library, forthcoming.   (56)

[251]   Taylor, John L. 1977. "Canada's North-West Indian Policy in the 1870's: Traditional Promises and Necessary Innovations." In *Approaches to Native History in Canada*, ed. D. A. Muise, pp. 104–10. National Museum of Man Mercury Series, History Division Paper no. 25. Ottawa: National Museums of Canada.   (49)

[252]   Tobias, John L. 1976. "Protection, Civilization, Assimilation: An Outline History of Canada's Indian Policy." *Western Canadian Journal of Anthropology* 61(2):13–30.   (2, 37, 45, 46)

[253]   ———. 1977. "Indian Reserves in Western Canada: Indian Homelands or Devices for Assimilation." In *Approaches to Native History in Canada*, ed. D. A. Muise, pp. 89–103. National Museum

of Man Mercury Series, History Division Paper no. 25. Ottawa: National Museums of Canada.   (49)

[254]   Tooker, Elizabeth. 1963. "The Iroquois Defeat of the Huron: A Review of Causes." *Pennsylvania Archaeologist* 33:115–23.   (10)

[255]   ———. 1964. *An Ethnography of the Huron Indians 1615–1649.* Bureau of American Ethnology Bulletin 190. Washington, D.C.: Government Printing Office. Reprinted, Midland, Ont.: Huronia Historical Development Council, 1967.   (10)

[256]   ———. 1978. *The Indians of the Northeast: A Critical Bibliography.* Bloomington and London: Indiana University Press for Newberry Library.   (4)

[257]   Torok, C. H. 1956. "The Tyendinaga Mohawks." *Ontario History* 57:69–77.   (26)

[258]   Torry, Alvin. 1864. *Autobiography of Rev. Alvin Torry, First Missionary to the Six Nations and the Northwestern Tribes of British North America.* Edited by Rev. William Hosmer. Auburn: W. J. Moses.   (32)

[259]   Trigger, Bruce G. 1959. "The Destruction of Huronia: A Study in Economic
and Cultural Change, 1609–1650."
*Transactions of the Royal Canadian Insti-
tute* 33(1):14–15.   (10)

[260]   ———. 1962. "The Historic Location
of the Hurons." *Ontario History*
54:137–48.   (10)

[261]   ———. 1965. "The Jesuits and the Fur
Trade." *Ethnohistory* 12:30–53.   (10)

[262]   ———. 1968. "The French Presence in
Huronia: The Structure of Franco-
Huron Relations in the First Half of the
Seventeenth Century." *Canadian Histori-
cal Review* 49:109–41.   (10)

*[263]   ———. 1971. "Champlain Judged by
His Indian Policy: A Different View of
Early Canadian History." *Anthropologica*,
n.s., 13:85–114.   (7)

[264]   ———. 1971. "The Mohawk-Mahican
War (1624–28): The Establishment of a
Pattern." *Canadian Historical Review*
52:276–86.   (10)

*[265]   ———. 1976. *The Children of Aataentsic:*

A History of the Huron People to 1660. 2 vols. Montreal and London: McGill-Queen's University Press. (10)

[266] Trudel, Marcel. 1960. *L'esclavage au Canada français: Histoire et conditions de l'esclavage.* Quebec: Presses de l'Université Laval. (13)

[267] Upton, Leslie F. S. 1973. "The Origins of Canadian Indian Policy." *Journal of Canadian Studies* 8:51–61. (33)

[268] ———. 1974. "Indian Affairs in Colonial New Brunswick." *Acadiensis* 3:3–26. (40)

[269] ———. 1975. "Colonists and Micmacs." *Journal of Canadian Studies* 10:44–56. (21, 40)

[270] ———. 1975. "Indian Policy in Colonial Nova Scotia, 1783–1871. *Acadiensis* 5:3–31. (40)

[271] ———. 1976. "Indians and Islanders: The Micmacs in Colonial Prince Edward Island." *Acadiensis* 6:21–42. (40)

[272] ———. 1977. "The Extermination of the Beothuks of Newfoundland." *Canadian Historical Review* 59:133–53. (41)

[273] ———. 1978. "The Beothuks: Questions and Answers." *Acadiensis* 7:150– 55.   (41)

[274] ———. 1979. *Micmacs and Colonists: Indian-White Relations in the Maritimes, 1713–1867*. Vancouver: University of British Columbia Press.   (21, 39, 40)

[275] Usher, Jean. 1971. "Apostles and Aborigines: The Social Theory of the Church Missionary Society." *Histoire Sociale–Social History* 7:28–52.   (32)

[276] ———. 1974. *William Duncan of Metlakatla: A Victorian Missionary in British Columbia*. National Museum of Man Publications in History, Paper no. 5. Ottawa: National Museums of Canada.   (54)

[277] Van Dusen, Conrad [Enemikeese]. 1867. *The Indian Chief: An Account of the Labours, Losses, Sufferings, and Oppression of Ke-zig-ko-e-ne-ne (David Sawyer), a Chief of the Ojibbeway Indians in Canada West*. London: William Nichols.   (33)

[278] Walker, James St. G. 1971. "The Indian in Canadian Historical Writing." *Canadian Historical Association Historical Papers* 1:21–51.   (3)

[279] Wallace, Anthony F. C. 1957. "Origins of Iroquois Neutrality: The Grand Settlement of 1701." *Pennsylvania History* 24:223–35. (16)

[280] Wallis, Wilson D., and Ruth S. Wallis. 1955. *The Micmac Indians of Eastern Canada*. Minneapolis: University of Minnesota Press. (19)

[281] Walsh, Gerald. 1971. *Indians in Transition: An Inquiry Approach*. Toronto: McClelland and Stewart. (59)

[282] Waubageshig [Harvey McCue], ed. 1970. *The Only Good Indian: Essays by Canadian Indians*. Toronto: New Press. (55)

[283] Weaver, Sally M. 1981. *Making Canadian Indian Policy: The Hidden Agenda, 1968–1970*. Toronto: University of Toronto Press. (56)

*[284] Weslager, C. A. 1978. *The Delawares: A Critical Bibliography*. Bloomington and London: Indiana University Press for Newberry Library. (4)

[285] Whiteside, Don. 1973. *Aboriginal People: A Selected Bibliography concerning Canada's First People*. Ottawa: National Indian Brotherhood. (3)

[286]   Wilson, J. Donald. 1974. "'No Blanket to Be Worn in School': The Education of Indians in Early Nineteenth Century Ontario." *Histoire Sociale–Social History* 7:293–305.   (36)

[287]   Wise, S. F. 1953. "The Indian Diplomacy of John Graves Simcoe." *Canadian Historical Association Report,* pp. 36–44.   (29)

[288]   ———. 1970. "The American Revolution and Indian History." In *Character and Circumstance: Essays in Honour of Donald Grant Creighton*, ed. John S. Moir. Toronto: Macmillan.   (24)

[289]   Wuttunee, William I. C. 1971. *Ruffled Feathers: Indians in Canadian Society.* Calgary: Bell Books.   (55)

[290]   Zoltvany, Yves F. 1964. "The Problem of Western Policy under Philippe de Rigaud de Vaudreuil (1703–1725)." *Canadian Historical Association Report*, pp. 9–24.   (17)

[291]   ———. 1965. "New France and the West, 1701–1713." *Canadian Historical Review* 46:301–22.   (17)

[292]   ———. 1967. "The Frontier Policy of Philippe de Rigaud de Vaudreuil, 1713–1725." *Canadian Historical Review* 48:227–50.   (17)

[293]   ———. 1974. *Philippe de Rigaud de Vaudreuil: Governor of New France, 1703–1725*. Toronto: McClelland and Stewart.   (17)

The Newberry Library
Center for the History of the American Indian
Founding Director: D'Arcy McNickle
Director: Francis Jennings

Established in 1972 by the Newberry Library, in conjunction with the Committee on Institutional Cooperation of eleven midwestern universities, the Center makes the resources of one of America's foremost research libraries in the Humanities available to those interested in improving the quality and effectiveness of teaching American Indian history. The Newberry's collections include some 110,000 volumes on the history of the American Indian and offer specialized resources for studying historical aspects of Indian-White relations and Indian linguistics. The Center also assists Native Americans engaged in writing tribal histories and developing educational materials.

ADVISORY COMMITTEE